T0320990

RISK-
RETURN
ANALYSIS

RISK-RETURN ANALYSIS

The Theory and Practice of Rational Investing

Volume III

HARRY M. MARKOWITZ

New York   Chicago   San Francisco   Athens   London
Madrid   Mexico City   Milan   New Delhi   Singapore
Sydney   Toronto

Copyright © 2020 by Harry M. Markowitz. All rights reserved. Printed in the United States of America. Except as permitted under the United States Copyright Act of 1976, no part of this publication may be reproduced or distributed in any form or by any means, or stored in a database or retrieval system, without prior written permission of the publisher.

1 2 3 4 5 6 7 8 9   LCR   25 24 23 22 21 20

ISBN: 978-0-07-181831-5
MHID: 0-07-181831-6

e-ISBN: 978-0-07-181833-9
e-MHID: 0-07-181833-2

This publication is designed to provide accurate and authoritative information in regard to the subject matter covered. It is sold with the understanding that neither the author nor the publisher is engaged in rendering legal, accounting, securities trading, or other professional services. If legal advice or other expert assistance is required, the services of a competent professional person should be sought.

—From a Declaration of Principles Jointly Adopted by
a Committee of the American Bar Association
and a Committee of Publishers and Associations

Library of Congress Cataloging-in-Publication Data
Markowitz, H. (Harry), 1927–
  Risk-return analysis : the theory and practice of rational investing vol. 3 / by Harry Markowitz.
     pages cm
  Includes bibliographical references.
  ISBN-13: 978-0-07-181831-5
  ISBN-10: 0-07-181831-6
  1. Investment analysis. 2. Investments—Mathematical models. 3. Portfolio management. II. Title.
  HG4529.M3755 2014
  332.6—dc23

2013018660

McGraw-Hill Education books are available at special quantity discounts to use as premiums and sales promotions, or for use in corporate training programs. To contact a representative, please visit the Contact Us page at www.mhprofessional.com.

[T]he race is not to the swift, nor the battle to the strong, neither yet bread to the wise, nor yet riches to men of understanding, nor yet favour to men of skill; but time and chance happeneth to them all.

—Ecclesiastes 9:11

Excuse me sir, but
How much longer would it take
If we did it right
The first time?

—Harry Max Markowitz

Life's tragedy is that
We get old too soon
And wise too late.

—Benjamin Franklin

If not now, when?
If not me, who?

—Hillel, the Elder

CONTENTS

PREFACE

This third volume of a four-volume book, *Risk-Return Analysis: The Theory and Practice of Rational Investing*, begins with Chapter 13. The subject matter of the present chapter was a *given*; the size of the actual chapter needed to adequately cover the topic, was a *variable*. It turned out that the requisite size was that of a small monograph. Chapter 14 is even larger, and is still very much "in process." It was therefore deemed best to first publish Chapter 13 on its own so that interested readers could begin the study of its contents.

As explained in the prefatory material of Volume I, the topics of the four volumes parallel the topics of the last four chapters of Markowitz (1959). Specifically, Volume I considers *single-period* decision analyses assuming *known odds* as did Markowitz (1959) Chapter 10. Volume II considers *many-period* analyses, still assuming *known odds,* as did Markowitz (1959) Chapter 11. The present volume is concerned with rational decision-making in the face of uncertainty, i.e., *when odds are not known,* as did Markowitz (1959) Chapter 12. The fourth volume will cover *application* matters not covered, or not adequately covered, in the prior three volumes. The chief difference between Chapter 13 of Markowitz (1959) and the planned Volume IV of this book, is that Markowitz (1959)

Chapter 13 was written *a priori*, when the world had no experience with the practical application of MVA (Mean Variance Analysis), whereas Volume IV of the present book is based on over a half-century of MVA experience.

Each volume of this book distinguishes between the actions of a hypothetical "Rational Decision Maker" (RDM) and those of a "Human Decision Maker" (HDM). Our focus is on rational—i.e., RDM—action, and HDM approximations to it. The reason that the HDM makes an appearance in these volumes at all, is because (as the subtitle of this book promises) the book deals with practice as well as theory. I do not mean by this the questionable practices documented in behavioral studies such as that of Odean (1999) or McKay (2013, 1841). Rather, I mean existing and proposed HDM practices that seek to emulate the behavior, and approximate the results, of the RDM. Discussions of this sort are scattered throughout the volumes of this book, including, but not only, Chapter 11 in Volume II, on "Judgment and Approximation."

THE RATIONAL DECISION MAKER

The RDM is a fictitious creation. Like other fictitious creations—such as the unicorn, or the fictional as opposed to the historical St. Nicholas—each storyteller can ascribe to it whatever attributes his or her audience can be persuaded are appropriate for the entity. The RDM of Mossin and Samuelson, discussed in Chapter 9, is a solitary investor. As Chapter 6 (in Volume II) spelled out in some detail, *my* RDM can be an individual (of either gender of course), a family, or an institution such as a university or symphony orchestra.

As a specific example, the frontice material of Volume II introduced a prototypical RDM as a family with husband, wife, four children, a dog, and a cat—all rational. But, as Markowitz (1959) emphasized, a rational entity is neither omniscient nor omnipotent. In particular, the rational cat cannot catch the irrational rat. This is perfectly plausible despite the fact that a hungry natural cat can eventually catch some natural rat. Presumably, our rational—but fussy, of course—cat would prefer to finish the tuna in its bowl than to eat a raw rat. Its moves toward catching the rat are perfunctory. Perhaps the Rational Cat (RC) does not really want to catch the Irrational Rat (IR) because it is a clean and sanitary white rat—saved by RC's good-hearted family from its fate in a research lab. Perhaps playing "cat and mouse" with IR is RC's only entertainment when the humanoid RDMs are out for the day, and either the RC or the Rational Dog (RD) is tired of playing hide and seek.

WORDS OF WISDOM

A friend of mine told me that when he got his copy of Volume II, he read my "Ode to Rationality" to his family, which they enjoyed, but they wondered why I chose a quote from the Rubàiyàt as my other offering. I explained why, and decided that it might be useful to the reader if I explained the reasons for my various frontice-page quotes.

The frontice page of Volume I contains an acknowledgment of the various members of Mrs. Markowitz's (the other Dr. Markowitz in our house) and my extensive family. Since then, our family has become even more extensive. Specifically, we now have a twentieth great grandchild, namely a boy whose first name is "Max," as is my middle name.

The frontice material of Volume II reflects its contents. As compared to Volume I, concerned with single-period decisions with known odds, Volume II adds a time dimension, as well as a risk dimension, to the analysis. It seemed to me that the quote from the *Rubàiyàt* perfectly captured the concepts of time and the dangers of the "real world." Its somber tone seemed to be a nice balance to the light-hearted "Ode." The implication of the pair of quotes is this: the world is a dangerous place, but try not to lose your sense of humor. As already noted, Volume III is concerned with rational action under uncertainty. Accordingly, it considers questions such as: what kinds of things can we know, how do we acquire such knowledge, and how should we act on the basis of this knowledge. In particular, how should one go about playing a successful game-of-life, and what's in for us to play our game-of-life in what is generally considered a moral manner. Such philosophical topics call for some philosophical quotes.

The first quote is from Ecclesiastes. It starts with "[T]he race is not to the swift," and ends with "But time and chance happeneth to them all." That could be the slogan of this entire, four-volume book.

The second offering on the frontice page concerns doing things right the first time. "Doing it right" does *not* mean insisting on perfection. It means *not* achieving appreciably less than time and resource constraints permit because of impatience. In the case of Chapter 13, to a large extent "doing it right" meant "doing it twice." Fortunately, I am blessed that Tony Batman (the CEO of 1st Global of Dallas, Texas, and sponsor of this book) and I share a common view of doing the present project right.

The Benjamin Franklin quote is sometimes paraphrased as

So soon old,
So late smart.

But the Franklin quote speaks of becoming "wise" rather than becoming "smart." One must distinguish *smartness* from *wiseness*, just as one must distinguish *wisdom* from *knowledge*. One speaks of "words of wisdom" and "volumes of knowledge," rather than "words of knowledge" and "volumes of wisdom." Note, however, that there is no wisdom without knowledge. Wisdom is only the final summing up: the inner insight.

The Hillel quote reminds me of the story of the Jewish sociology professor who sought the reason for a common Jewish mannerism. He asked his rabbi, who sent the professor to an older and wiser rabbi, who sent him to a still older and wiser rabbi, etc., until the professor sat, in the "old country," in the presence of the oldest and wisest rabbi. The professor asked, "Wise old rabbi, why is it that when you ask a Jew a question, he answers with another question?" The wise old rabbi transfixed the professor with a pointing finger and an intense gaze, and said, "Why not?"

The use by Jews of questions for purposes other than interrogation can have serious objectives. The quote form Hillel asked "when" and "who." The answer is *not* always "me," "right now." For example, the first Monday of December, my colleagues (Mary "Midge" McDonald and Lilli Alexander) and I meet to discuss which tasks must be done before December 15 (when Christmas cards should be in the mail), which before December 25, which before December 31, and which may be done the following year. We also make sure that everyone knows who will do what. In addition to "who" and "when" other important questions include "what," "how," and "why." The use by Jews of questions for noninterrogatory purposes is ancient. In particular, Hillel, the Elder, died in 10 A.D., and is said to have lived 120 years, just like Moses. Conceivably, the noninterrogatory use of questions had been passed down from biblical times.

Benjamin Franklin did not offer wisdom in the form of questions, but he knew the value of questions of various sorts. He had a saying, which I will amplify a bit, to the effect that

He who knows *how*,
Will be supervised by
He who knows *what* and *when*;
Who will be employed by

He who knows *why*.

JOHN VON NEUMANN

How has this book stood on von Neumann's shoulders? "Let me count the ways:"

Volume I centered on mean-variance approximations to *expected utility*. The expected utility max was proposed by Daniel Bernoulli (1954, 1738) as an alternative to the clearly faulty expected return, or expected win or loss, rule. But it remained only a plausible heuristic until von Neumann and Morgenstern (1944) presented an axiomatic justification for it.

This set of axioms opened a floodgate of applications, extensions and reexaminations. Volume I, as just noted, seeks to establish the range of applicability of MV analysis by examining theoretically and empirically the ability for such analysis to approximate the expected values of various utility functions, including Bernoulli's logarithmic utility.

The natural extension of von Neumann's axiomatic justification of the utility analysis of action in the face of risk (known odds) is the L. J. Savage (1954) axiomatic defense of the EU/PB (expected return/personal probability) maximum for choice under uncertainty.

This, in turn, produced the Bayesian revolution which has completely turned around most scholar's view of statistical inference, both formal—the way people work with numbers—and informal—the way many (including me) view any learning process. The other consequence of von Neumann's defense of expected utility has been the re-creation of alternative axiom systems deemed superior as *prescriptive* of desirable behavior, or descriptive of risk-facing behavior, such as Kahneman and Tversky's (1979) prospect theory, from which Behavior Finance" sprang. Also, Allais' (1953) was the first to question the conclusions and therefore the premises, of von Neumann's analysis. This resulted in hierarchical utility, to be discussed at length in Chapter 15.

Volume II is centered on Decision Support Systems (DSSs) which help the family—or other enterprise—play its **Game of Life**. Of course "*Game*" here refers to von Neumann's "Game Theory," as published in von Neumann (1928), and more completely in von Neumann and Morgenstern (1944). I consider the latter to be the fourth modern economic paradigm, including those of Adam Smith (2003, 1776), Karl Marx (2010, 1867), John Maynard Keynes (2011, 1936). Von Neumann's contribution to economics is not confined to the game theory. It also includes optimum growth paths (von Neumann 1945–1946). Von Neumann made frequent visits to the Cowles Commission for Research in Economics, unfortunately for me, long before I arrived at Cowles. In particular, at the 50th Anniversary of the Cowles Commission, Lawrence Klein reviewed recent work on models of the U. S. and other economics. He was asked how his models differed from his Nobel-Prize winning work reported in Klein (1950). Klein described how the modern computer made all the difference. Rather than having equations to characterize the entire U. S.

economy, he now had hundreds of equations and variables to trace out micro-relationships.

At the point Tjalling Koopmans signaled, in his quiet way, that he would like to say a few words. Koopmans reminisced that during WWII, von Neumann would frequently travel by train from Washington, D.C. to Los Alamos—with a stop-over in Chicago, so that von Neumann could visit the Cowles Commission. The latter would expect von Neumann to share with them his latest insights into game theory or growth optimal paths. Instead, von Neumann told them about a machine he was working on that could do thousands of calculations per minute. According to Koopmans, no one at the Cowles Commission could see any way that a machine that could do thousands of calculations per minute could ever be of any use to economics.

ACKNOWLEDGMENTS

I would very much like to thank those who sponsored this work and/or read it cover-to-cover and advised on its contents. These include Tony Batman, Ken Blay, Roger Brown, John Guerard and Alasdar Mullarney.

I also want to express my thanks to and love for my wife Barbara. Barbara is suffering from the after-effects of a stroke, but otherwise we are both in our nineties and in good health. She still recognizes me. In particular, after dinner each night (she needs to be fed of course), I take her hand and ask her if she recognizes me, her husband Harry. She nods yes and we reminisce. She cannot speak because of the stroke but nods her head and acknowledges with her eyes.

RISK-
RETURN
ANALYSIS

13

PREDECESSORS

INTRODUCTION

As explained in the Preface, this third volume of a four-volume book presents the theory of rational decision-making when *odds are not known*. Its central concern is how to go rationally from *information* to *action*. Here I use "information" in the broadest sense, including, e.g., not only computerized data (with errors of course), but also news reports of varying credibility and relevant third-party analyses whose methodology may be well-documented or not. "Action" means different things to different people. To family planners, action includes major decisions concerning their families' "game of life," including deciding which of conflicting reports to believe on the health benefits of various foods, and to what extent to trade taste preferences for healthy-eating. For the nutritional scientist, action includes the design of nutritional experiments and the interpretation of their results. For designers of financial decision support systems, action includes selecting "investables" (e.g., asset classes or individual securities), and a methodology for estimating their relevant return parameters.

Typically, current action as a function of current information depends on lessons learned in the past. Some of these lessons are inferences from one's own experience. Others are alleged facts offered by others, such as parents, friends, how-to articles, and TV ads—i.e., slivers of the collective (often contradictory) experience of all of mankind. Some lessons are simple IF/THEN rules such as

IF you are not careful when changing a light bulb,

THEN you may get an electric shock.

Other lessons involve more complex hypotheses, such as, "If you add up the calories you consume, subtract the calories you expend, and the difference is positive, you will gain weight."

This book's subtitle speaks of "theory and practice." "Practice" does not necessarily only mean "how things are done now." It also includes proposals for improving practice, such as the Markowitz and van Dijk proposal for portfolio selection in a changing world, described in Chapter 11 (in Volume II); "Tax Cognizant Portfolio Analysis" (TCPA), also described in Chapter 11; and data-summary techniques for "remote Bayesians," described and illustrated in Chapter 5, Volume I, and the like. The general approach used in the various volumes of this book is to deduce what an RDM (Rational Decision Maker) would do in a given situation and how an HDM (Human Decision Maker) could emulate the RDM's actions and results. The central questions for the present volume, therefore, are:

A. By what principles would an RDM go from information—including relevant nonquantitative information as well as numerical data—to investment and other game-of-life decisions?

B. How can HDMs and their DSSs (Decision Support Systems) apply these principles, at least approximately?

Question A, as to how an RDM would act when odds are not known, as a function of current information and (someone's) prior experience, may itself be rephrased as three basic philosophical questions, namely:

1. What kinds of things can we know?
2. How can we come by this knowledge?
3. How should we act based on this (perhaps very limited) knowledge?

These are questions with which great minds have struggled for centuries. Some (such as Plato, Aristotle, Descartes, Hume, Kant, and Charles Sanders Peirce) might identify themselves as "philosophers." Others (such as R. A. Fisher, E. L. Neyman and Karl Pearson, and Leonard J. Savage) might identify their professions otherwise. But all have thought deeply about these questions.

I began reading philosophy when I was in high school, long before I developed portfolio theory in pursuit of a PhD degree. (See Les Prix Nobel 1990.) I was particularly struck by the works of Descartes and Hume. Their views—and the trains of thought they triggered—influenced my approach to investment, and still do. But the greatest influences in the formation of my views of these matters came later, in the works of J. von Neumann and O. Morgenstern (1944) and Leonard J. Savage (1954). The former was cited extensively in Volume II; the latter, as well as the former, are central to the present volume.

The present chapter reviews the positions of Descartes, Hume, Kant and others, and my current views vis-à-vis them. It is not intended to be a balanced account of the history of philosophy, but primarily an informal account of my own fundamental views on the preceding three numbered questions. For example, I do not explain Plato's views and then proceed to explain why; instead, I am a disciple of Aristotle, as amended by Hume, Galileo, Newton, Darwin, Hilbert, etc. Such a discussion would not advance the objectives I have for this chapter.

Newton famously said that "I saw so far because I stood on the shoulders of giants." I would add that those who do not study their relevant predecessors stand on the ground. Those who learn from their predecessors stand on the shoulders of giants, who stood on the shoulders of a succession of giants stretching back—literally—thousands of years. I have learned much from the giants reviewed in this chapter, albeit a small fraction of what they have to teach.

RENÉ DESCARTES

In his first meditation, titled "About the Things We May Doubt," Descartes (1968,1641) notes:

Everything I have accepted up to now as being absolutely true and assured, I have learned from or through the senses. But I have sometimes found that these senses played me false, and it is prudent never to trust entirely those who have once deceived us.

He says, for example, that he may be dreaming:

It certainly seems to me at the moment that I am not looking at this paper with my eyes closed; that this head that I shake is not asleep; that I hold out this hand intentionally and deliberately; and that I am aware of it . . . I recall having often been deceived in sleep by similar illusions. . . .

After further reflections, he concludes:

This is why perhaps that, from this, we shall not be wrong in concluding that physics, astronomy, medicine, and all the other sciences which depend on the consideration of composite things are most doubtful and uncertain, but that arithmetic, geometry, and the other sciences of this nature, which deal only with very simple and general things, without bothering about their existence or nonexistence, contain something certain and indubitable. For whether I am awake or sleeping, two and three added together always make five, and a square never has more than four sides;

and it does not seem possible that truths so apparent can be suspected of any falsity or uncertainty.

But Descartes challenges these supposed certainties, saying:

I shall suppose, therefore, that there is not a true God, who is the sovereign source of truth, but some evil demon, no less cunning and deceiving than power-ful, who has used all his artifice to deceive me. I will suppose that the heavens, the air, the earth, colors, shapes, sounds and all external things that we see are only illusions and deceptions which he uses to take me in.

In particular, Descartes's "evil demon" may cause him to err in any deductions he makes concerning algebra or geom-etry. Perhaps (by implication) his most enduring creation, "Analytic Geometry," now universally taught on its own or in precalculus, is erroneous, and the people for whom he is writ-ing these meditations do not exist.

So that, after having thought carefully about it, and having scrupulously examined everything, one must then, in conclusion, take as assured that the proposi-tion: I am, I exist, is necessarily true, every time I express it or conceive of it in my mind.

Or, as he puts it, originally in French, in his "Discourse on Method" (1968, 1637), "cogito ergo sum"—*I think, therefore I am.*

Is Descartes Practical?

Let us turn now from issues such as how do we know that the world we see is not an illusion created by an evil demon to whether Descartes-like concerns are applicable to practical matters such as financial practice. Financial practice is built on *facts*, such as those reported in the earnings reports of the *Wall Street Journal* (WSJ). For example, consider a specific such fact, such as a specific earnings report published in a specific WSJ issue. Maybe that number is a misprint; maybe it's a lie; maybe it is an honest mistake. These things happen. How should that affect our actions?

If you wish to think clearly about the first two numbered questions in the Introduction to this chapter—namely, "What kinds of things can we know?" and "How are we to come by this knowledge?"—I recommend that you (at some reflective moment, in the quiet of your study, or while walking on a pleasant day) do a Descartes-like exercise, "About the Things We May Doubt." The next few sections present the conclusions of my own Descartes-like exercise, not done in one evening as Descartes alleges for each of his meditations, but on and off over many years. I make no claim that any of the conclusions I reached are "original," i.e., that no one else has come to, and perhaps published, essentially the same bundle of conclusions.

THERE IS NO "IS," ONLY "WAS" AND "WILL BE"

Descartes says that if we seek certainty, we must ignore sense experience—even the sensations that are before us at the moment—because the senses have sometimes lied to us, and how can we trust a witness who sometimes does not tell the truth? How much more must Descartes distrust memory? If he does not trust the sense impressions before him now, how could he trust the memory of a scene a year or a month ago, or even a minute ago? For example, in the movie *Gigi* the Maurice Chevalier character sings the song "I Remember It Well" to the Hermione Gingold character:

Honoré (Maurice Chevalier)
and Mamita (Hermione Gingold)

H: We met at nine
M: We met at eight
H: I was on time
M: No, you were late
H: Ah, yes, I remember it well
We dined with friends
M: We dined alone
H: A tenor sang
M: A baritone
H: Ah, yes, I remember it well
That dazzling April moon!
M: There was none that night
And the month was June

H: That's right. That's right.
M: It warms my heart to know that you
remember still the way you do
H: Ah, yes, I remember it well

"I Remember It Well"
From *Gigi* (1958)
(Lyrics: Alan Jay Lerner/Frederick Loewe)

Honoré here has a problem with a long-term memory. But short-term memory is also imperfect, such as occasions when one walks into a room to get something and forgets what it was to be gotten. Clearly, both long- and short-term memories are at least as questionable as immediate sense sensations.

But I will argue that without memory there can be neither observation nor thought. In particular, the so-called "perception of the moment" is in fact a combination of short-term memory *and* often a prediction of the near future. For example, suppose that *precisely* on the minute I started writing

Four score and seven years ago . . .

Suppose further that, at *precisely* π (= 3.1416 . . .) seconds after the minute, my pen-tip was at the top of the loop that forms the letter "o" in "ago." What was I thinking about at *precisely* π seconds after the minute? Probably my sight was focused on the pen-tip. But, while at some level I remembered what I was trying to do, I probably wasn't "thinking" about the writing of the letter "o" but perhaps about the remainder of the phrase still to be written. The writing process itself was on "automatic."

The "perception" of the world at a literal instant often includes a forecast of the near future as well as a memory of the recent past. In the case of writing the letter "o," my mind "remembers" how my pen will continue beyond the apex of the letter. This memory is not in the front of my consciousness, but it is there.

For another example, consider a moving object in the environment—not something one controls, such as the pentip—but something beyond one's control, such as an object now falling from a shelf due to a small earthquake tremor. It seems to me that before it hits the ground, one or more of the mind's parallel processors (described in Chapter 12, Volume II) will have calculated the object's trajectory, whether it poses a risk to anyone or anything, including the object itself, and what the likely economic consequences are to any objects at risk. In general, whether a process involves one's own volition (like the swinging of a tennis racket) or an object not controlled by one's mind, such as a fast-approaching tennis ball, each literal instant—*not* short *interval*, such as a microsecond, but literal instant—is "defined" by the mind's memories and forecasts.

Without a *memory* of what it is you are thinking about, there can be no *thought*. Once a thought-stream starts, thinking about something is a process that includes a *memory* of what you have just thought about already **and** a *memory* of where you are headed, i.e., a prediction of, or directive as to, what the thinking process is aiming at. One symptom of early-stage Alzheimer's is the loss of short-term memory. If Descartes had had early-stage Alzheimer's, he might have written: "I think, therefore . . . ? Hey! Who am I writing this for anyway?"

The *prediction* that the loose object will fall toward the ground is the consequence of one of many hypotheses one's mind has concerning how the world works. Let us consider the nature of such hypotheses.

WORKING HYPOTHESES

One could not survive if one insisted on certainty before every action. If nothing else, one would starve to death for fear that all foods contain some agonizing poison. One needs *working hypotheses* to live, prosper, and write a book. For example, Descartes said that the existence of other minds (in other human beings) was subject to doubt. In fact, his third meditation, titled "Of God, That He Exists," argued that other than his own existence, which was certain, the proposition that was *closest* to being certain was the existence of God. The existence of other humans was less certain. But Descartes (1993, 1641) wrote and *published* his *Meditations*. When I ship a volume of a book to its publisher, it is under the assumption that other people exist, and some of them might even read my work. I assume that the same was true when Descartes shipped his *Meditations* to his publisher. It must have been a working hypothesis of his.

In Chapter 12 (in Volume II), I argued that the mind works as if its memories were assigned to "representatives" (or "reps") who, among other things, monitor the goings-on at the conscious level, and speak out (at least to a mental "committee") when the rep deems that one of its memories is relevant to the moment, as illustrated by the popping-up in my mind of the line "Double double toil and trouble" when I read the word "double" on a sandwich brought in because of my tight schedule. Here I note that, among the memories assigned to reps, are working hypotheses about various aspects of the world, including who we are, what we are currently doing, how we make a living, and how all this fits into the broader picture we carry with us concerning "me and the world." Small subsets of these innumerable working hypotheses are assumed at any moment in order for us to be able to act from moment to moment.

Among my own innumerable working hypotheses are, for example, that if the world has a finite age, it is more likely to be a few billion years old than a few thousand years old. I believe this in part from things I have read—such as Darwin's *Origin of Species* and popular accounts of the Big Bang—and partly from my memory of the sight of huge dinosaur skeletons at Chicago's Field Museum of Natural History. I also believe, for various reasons, that continents shift, the theory of relativity has upset the classical notions of time and space, and quantum theory has upset our notion of location and momentum. At a different level, I believe that fire burns, water quenches thirst, things I call "food" satisfy hunger (some being tastier than others), my skin separates me from not-me, and I can *will* certain movements by "me" but cannot similarly move—by willing it—things outside me. Working hypotheses that guide my day-to-day actions include

- The existence of various individuals with characteristics such as their tastes and abilities;
- The general nature of the room or street behind me, and consequently the meaning of the sounds of objects I do not see, such as an approaching car;
- "Five times six is thirty," and the rest of the multiplication table that I memorized as a child;
- I often make errors in adding up a column of numbers, but, whether I get the right answer or not, every such arithmetical problem has a unique correct answer;

and countless other purported facts of mathematics, science, history, financial theory, and personal experience—including assorted facts and values I learned from my parents, friends, radio, TV and the printed word. Any of these may be assumed at any appropriate time, either in my thought-stream or in my actions. For example, when I walk from Point A to Point B after having a conscious thought, "I should take a sweater," I subconsciously remember where the sweater is (usually), the path to it, and how footsteps are executed. These—explicitly, or in effect—are working hypotheses of mine.

Typically then, I act as if I knew for sure a set of currently relevant hypotheses. There are exceptions, as in a game of cards when I do not know my opponent's cards or in reading a mystery story when I mentally cycle through hypotheses as to which suspect is the murderer. But more typically, I take a set of currently relevant hypotheses for granted, without question, as if certain. For example, I drive as if I were sure that there was no gaping sinkhole over the next hill or around the imminent curve. I could never get anywhere if I did not.

For the most part, my working hypotheses are "sometimes in error but never in doubt"—at least they are not in doubt at the time I take action based on them, e.g., in driving or in recalling "the world according to science." But scientific theories change. Often what was taught us in school we later learn has been found not to be so. For example, I have a clear picture in my head of the atom as a miniature solar system with electrons whizzing around a relatively heavy nucleus, and I also recall reading that this model is now obsolete. We drive making assumptions—such as there being no gaping sinkholes and no cars running red lights—and when these hypotheses are in error, there are accidents.

There are hypotheses I know to be false, but I act as if they are true. For example, each day I assume that I will live at least one more day, although I know that someday that will not be true. That is why I have an estate plan. I also know that an intercontinental nuclear war is not beyond the realm of possibility, but I am among the majority who have elected *not* to build a place where I can live while the radioactive dust settles. In other words, as a working hypothesis I assume that the event has zero probability of happening. I similarly act as if there is no chance that markets (including the stock market) will cease to function for any appreciable length of time, e.g., because of an enemy or terrorist attack or our own political folly.

Some "certainties" are more certain than others. For example, I would be shocked if I rounded a blind corner and encountered a car-size sinkhole, but not half as shocked as I would be if I found that Godzilla was about to stomp on my car. Some hypotheses must necessarily be true if others are true. For example, the truth of the hypothesis that a particular individual can be counted on to perform a certain task implies the truth of the hypothesis that other people exist.

Typically (perhaps inevitably), a hypothesis has no truth by itself alone, but only when combined with other hypotheses. For example, an article in a financial-economics journal (and a lot of other journals as well) may conclude that Phenomenon A causes Phenomenon B, without reminding the reader that the relationship is *assumed* to be linear, that the residual term is *assumed* to be uncorrelated with the "independent" variable, that the data are *assumed* to be without error, and that the residual term is *assumed* to have a particular (often Gaussian) distribution—not to mention that perhaps A and B may go up and down together because B causes A, or both are related to another factor.

The simultaneous assertion that A causes B, and not vice versa, *and* that the relationship between them is linear, *and* that the estimation error is Gaussian and independent of changes in B is called a "joint hypothesis." Another example of a joint hypothesis is provided in a noteworthy book by a leading mathematician/physicist at the turn of the nineteenth-to-twentieth centuries. In his Chapter 5 on "Experiment and Geometry," Henri Poincaré (1902) astutely argues that physical observations are joint hypotheses involving both physics and geometry, and therefore the objective truth of Euclidean geometry cannot be proved or refuted. Specifically, he tells us:

> If [Nicholaus] Lobatschewsky's geometry is true, the parallax of a very distant star will be finite. If [Bernhard] Riemann's is true, it will be negative. These are the results which seem within the reach of experiment, and it is hoped that astronomical observations may enable us to decide between the two geometries. But what we call a straight line in astronomy is simply the path of a ray of light. If, therefore, we were to discover negative parallaxes, or to prove that all parallaxes are higher than a certain limit, we should have a choice between two conclusions: We could give up Euclidean geometry, or we could modify the laws of optics and suppose that light is not rigorously propagated in a straight line. It is needless to add that everyone would look upon this latter solution as the more advantageous. Euclidean geometry, therefore, has nothing to fear from fresh experiments.

This was written not long before Albert Einstein concluded that the simplest explanation of gravitational observations included the hypothesis that matter distorted space-time like a bowling ball would distort the surface of a mattress. Part of Einstein's genius was his ability to recognize and reconsider long-standing hypotheses which everyone else took for granted.

The result of Charles Peirce's Descartes-like exercise is similar to, but different from, my own. Specifically, Peirce (1955a–c, 1908) said:

> *Philosophers of very diverse stripes propose that philosophy shall take its start from one or another state of mind in which no man, least of all a beginner in philosophy, actually is. One proposes that you shall begin by doubting everything, and says that there is only one thing that you cannot doubt, as if doubting were "as easy as lying." Another proposes that we should begin by observing "the first impressions of sense," forgetting that our very percepts are the results of cognitive elaboration. But in truth, there is but one state of mind from which you can "set out," namely, the very state of mind in which you actually find yourself at the time you do "set out"—a state in which you are laden with an immense mass of cognition already formed, of which you cannot divest yourself if you would; and who knows whether, if you could, you would not have made all knowledge impossible to yourself? . . . [R]ecognize, as you must, that there is much that you do not doubt in the least. Now that which you do not at all doubt, you must and do regard as infallible, absolute truth.*

I agree with Peirce that I have no choice but to start with "the state of mind" in which I find myself. This includes innumerable working hypotheses, some of which I consider as virtual certainties. I note, however, that what one person may consider a virtual certainty may be doubted by another and that some things which almost everyone considers a virtual certainty in one generation may be considered antiquated by another. Surely, action should be tempered by the virtual certainty that some hypotheses I do not question "today," I will reject "tomorrow."

The Ultimate Descartes, Assuming There Was a Descartes

This seems to be the ultimate conclusion of René Descartes's line of reasoning:

> *What is, won't happen exactly that way again, and*
> *What was, won't happen exactly the same again;*
> *In fact, the is, is gone before you can say "is."*
> *So what is, won't happen, because what we call is,*
> *Isn't is, it's was,*
> *And the was won't happen,*
> *And what won't happen, won't happen.*
> *So what you think was and what you think will be,*
> *Are the only is's.*
> *The rest are "working hypotheses,"*
> *Which sometimes work,*
> *And sometimes don't.*

RDM REASONING

As has already been noted, frequently, this book postulates rational decision makers (RDMs) who differ from human decision makers (HDMs) (a) in having no fuzziness in their perception of their own preferences, (b) in making no errors in logic, and (c) in having unlimited computing and memory capabilities. It will be convenient to assume (for HDMs who are rational enough to be readers of this book), there is a unique associated RDM, and conversely for each RDM there is a unique associated HDM. Possibly, there may be two HDMs, or two RDMs, or both, who are identical. My only assumption is that it is meaningful to speak of the "*RDM associated with its HDM*" and the "*HDM associated with its RDM.*"

Concerning the specification that the RDMs make no errors of logic, Aristotelian scholars combined six of Aristotle's works on logic into a major work they called the Organon. The third and fourth books of the Organon, respectively called the *Prior Analytics* and the *Posterior Analytics*, are concerned, respectively, with "deductive" and "inductive" reasoning. As I will detail later, Aristotle's analysis of "deductive reasoning" is the foundation of today's formal logic. But Aristotle's analysis of "inductive reasoning" came crashing down with the work of our next philosopher.

DAVID HUME

According to Hume (2009, 1740), page 354:

All the objects of human reason or enquiry may natu-rally be divided into two kinds, to wit, "Relations of Ideas," and "Matters of Fact." Of the first kind are the sciences of Geometry, Algebra, and Arithmetic; and, in short, every affirmation which is either intuitively or demonstratively certain. That the square of the hypotenuse is equal to the square of the two sides, is a proposition which expresses a relation between these figures. That three times five is equal to the half of thirty expresses a relation between these numbers. Propositions of this kind are discoverable by the mere operation of thought, without dependence on what is anywhere existent in the universe. Though there never were a circle or triangle in nature, the truths demonstrated by Euclid would forever retain their certainty and evidence.

Matters of fact, which are the second objects of human reason, are not ascertained in the same man-ner, nor is our evidence of their truth, however great, of a like nature with the forgoing. The contrary of every matter of fact is still possible; because it can never imply a contradiction and is conceived by the mind with the same facility and distinctness, as if ever so conformable to reality. That the sun will not rise tomorrow is no less intelligible a proposition, and implies no more contradiction than the affirmation, that it will rise. We should in vain, therefore, attempt to demonstrate its falsehood. Were it demonstrably false, it would imply a contradiction and could never be distinctly conceived by the mind.

Relationships of Ideas

Hume uses geometry as an example of what he calls "relations of ideas." For Hume, geometry meant Euclid: Non-Euclidean geometry was a thing of the future. Central to the writings of Euclid was the concept of a *proof.* He started from unproven statements which he called axioms, postulates and definitions. From these he deduced other statements by a sequence of intermediate statements. Each step in this sequence had a justification—a reason why that particular step was permitted. Modern mathematical texts often omit steps or omit the reason a given step is permitted. This may make the text seem more readable, but it often leaves readers puzzled as to how one is to get *rigorously* from Point A to Point B in the argument. In any case, unless a rigorous proof could be supplied, the assertion is unproven.

In the second half of the nineteenth century, leading mathematicians began to differ sharply as to what should be the basic axioms of mathematics and what steps should be permitted in proofs. This is of practical consequence since, for example, modern probability theory is built on premises and permitted logical steps that some distinguished nineteenth-century mathematicians forbade.

Euclid's magnificent systematic account of essentially all mathematics known to the Greeks at the time, including number theory as well as geometry, makes a basic *expository* error that none of the modern logic-systems would permit. Specifically, Euclid begins his elements with the following definitions:

- A *point* is that which has no part;
- A *line* is breadthless length; etc.

The problem here (e.g.) is that the word "point" is defined using the word "part," but the word "part" is undefined. Any attempt to rectify this problem by defining "part" would lead to either an infinite regress or a circular definition.[1] None of Euclid's proofs do, in fact, rely on these so-called definitions.

Note 1 samples Hilbert's (1971, 1899) rigorous—but obtuse—reformulation of the "foundations" of geometry, i.e., its initial steps instead of Euclid's "definitions." Neither Hilbert's work, nor any of the late nineteenth- and early twentieth-century debates over which axioms and what kinds of deductive steps should be permitted, challenge the magnitude and importance of Euclid's achievement. Nor do any of these modern refinements invalidate Hume's basic observation, that mathematical "truths" are the relationships among ideas as demonstrated by deductive reasoning.

Matters of Fact

I raise a paperweight off my desk and release it. It falls to the desk. I lift it again, release it, and again it falls to the desk. I do this several times, always with the same result. One could build an industrial robot that would lift and release the paperweight day and night. It could have a sensor that would sound an alarm if the weight did not fall, and make a record of the event in case no one was around to hear the alarm. The robot's counter might tell us that the weight has been raised and released 100,000 times, and it fell each time. Sir Isaac Newton told us that the motion of the moon around the Earth can be explained by assuming that the Earth and moon attract each other by an inverse square law. But these laws also explain the Earth going around the sun, billions of suns rotating around our galaxy, and billions of galaxies with their motions through vast empty space, as well as an apple or paperweight falling toward the earth.

Question: If 10^9 galaxies with 10^9 stars obey Newton's laws, do these 10^{18} observations *prove with certainty* that Newton's "Universal" laws hold *universally*? Of course not, since—if Hume's philosophical argument did not convince us otherwise—we know now that Einstein's General Relativity hypothesis explains everything that Newton's hypothesis explained, plus phenomena that Newton's hypothesis failed to explain, e.g., why Mercury's motion did not quite conform to Newton's law. In addition, Einstein's theory predicts phenomena no one previously anticipated, namely the bending of light rays toward massive bodies such as the sun.

But Hume wrote more than a century before the creation and confirmation of general relativity, as well as before the triumph of quantum mechanics, whose predictions would have seemed as bizarre to eighteenth-century thinkers as would a ball occasionally falling up rather than down. Hume's argument (in passages not reproduced here) was simply that he could not conceive of a proof that *demonstrated* that anything about the perceived world—that could be imagined—could *not* happen.

Value Judgments

Hume also said that value judgments cannot be deduced "by reason." For example, in the first paragraph of Item 5 in "Appendix I—Concerning Moral Sentiment" in his *An Enquiry Concerning the Principles of Morals*, Hume (1983, 1751) tells us:

> *It appears evident, that the ultimate ends of human actions can never, in any case, be accounted for by reason, but recommend themselves entirely to the sentiments and affections of mankind, without any dependence on the intellectual faculties.*

In Section I, "Of the General Principles of Morals," in the same volume, after reviewing arguments as to the roles of "reason" and "sentiment" in moral judgments, Hume ascribes moral judgments to " . . . some internal sense or feeling, which nature has made universal in the whole species." Perhaps if Hume lived now, when some men and women consider it their moral duty to do great harm to many who mean them no harm, Hume might have questioned whether the "moral sentiments" which he saw expressed, at that time, in that place, in his crowd, were in fact "universal in the whole species."

Hume was quite impatient with views contrary to his on this matter. In particular, he says:

> *Disputes with men, pertinaciously obstinate in their principles, are, of all others, the most irksome; except, perhaps, those with persons, entirely disingenuous, who really do not believe the opinions they defend, but engage in the controversy, from affectation, from a spirit of opposition, or from a desire of showing with an ingenuity, superior to the rest of mankind.*
>
> . . .
>
> *Those who have denied the reality of moral distinctions, may be ranked among the disingenuous disputants; nor is it conceivable that any human creature could ever seriously believe that all characters and actions were alike entitled to the affection and regard of everyone.*
>
> . . .
>
> *Let a man's insensibility be ever so great, he must often be touched with the images of RIGHT and WRONG; and let his prejudices be ever so obstinate, he must observe, that others are susceptible of like impressions.*

While I share Hume's values, and truly hate to be thought of as being a "human creature" to be lumped with other "disingenuous disputants," I really *do* side with those who say that there is no universally accepted principle that would settle all value disputes, were all people to understand this principle. Even among those who abhor the idea of a suicide bomber, there are great value differences, e.g., concerning abortion, the eating of animals, and the transfer of wealth from the rich to the poor. In different times and places even, men whom we greatly admire took for granted practices upon which we now frown. In particular, the economic system of Plato's and Aristotle's Greece was based on the use of slaves. Not only were slaves used in agriculture, as they were in the antebellum U.S. South, but they were the butchers, the bakers, and the cobblers of the day. They filled all jobs beneath the dignity of a "free man," roughly equivalent to "a gentleman" in the Old South.

The fact that value judgments cannot be proved deductively, or confirmed or refuted empirically, does not mean that they have no role in a many-volume book whose goal to help goal-seeking entities (including individuals, families and institutions) play their game-of-life. Altruistic *actions*—not just "feelings," but *actions*—include (1) gifts and other thoughtful acts to family, friends and charitable institutions and (2) one's instructions for the disposition of one's estate to family, to others who have been close or helpful, and to one's favorite "good causes." More generally, I observe that most people seek to live an admirable life. Few of us choose to devote ourselves to helping others in the manner of Mother Teresa, but most people want to be thought well of by friends, family and neighbors. Man is a social animal who evolved to both feel and exert social pressure, for the survival of the species.

It is not true that all investors seek high mean for given risk and low risk for given mean return, and in any case, I cannot *prove* that they *should* have these goals. Nevertheless, I observed that many investors have such goals, and I among others have built careers helping investors to achieve these goals. Similarly, it seems clear to me that there are typical goals in the playing of the game-of-life, and that quantitative and computer methods can help households achieve some of these goals. As to the nature of the ultimate goals in playing the game-of-life, I think that, basically, Aristotle had it right.

EUDAIMONIA

Sometimes a concept that is well-named in one language has no counterpart in another. In particular, it is sometimes useful to introduce words-without-counterparts into technical discussions. For example, all SIMSCRIPTs distinguish between "exogenous" and "endogenous" events. After the SIMSCRIPT language specification process was no longer under my control, someone introduced "external" and "internal" as synonyms, respectively, of "exogenous" and "endogenous." But "exogenous," for example, does *not* mean "external" or "on the outside." It means "*from* the outside." E.g., if one views the Earth and its atmosphere as the system-under-discussion, then the arrival of the world-changing comet that lead to the end of the dominance of the dinosaurs was a world-changing *exogenous* event, *from* the outside.

Aristotle speaks of *eudaimonia* as the goal of the rational individual. *Eudaimonia* is often translated as "happiness," but the latter is a very poor translation of the former. For example, a few decades ago many U.S. adults were happy in their choice of cigarette, until the Surgeon General said they might get cancer from it. The entertainer Ted Lewis had a catch phrase, "Is everybody *happy*?" But that clearly referred to happiness for the moment, whereas *eudaimonia* denotes a life of joy and sorrow, struggle and triumph, perhaps family, surely good friends, and the thought that one will be well remembered after one is gone, if only in the memories of one's children and grandchildren.

The perfect example of what might be called "*eudaimonia* lost, *eudaimonia* found," is Charles Dickens's "A Christmas Carol." Ebenezer Scrooge might have been happy in his miserliness, since he took great pleasure in accumulating wealth. But the ghosts of the past, present and future showed him some past, present and future consequences of his actions, such as the medical condition of poor Tiny Tim, Scrooge's fiancé Belle leaving him because he loved money more than he loved her, and the shabby way he will be remembered after his death. Fortunately, the lesson sank in, in time for him to become a loving, caring person, and as a consequence—like a moral law of action and reaction—he was blessed with *eudaimonia*.

Recurring themes in Volume II included the portfolio selection context, portfolio selection as social choice, the objectives of the "player" in his or her game-of-life, and whether mortal man's decision support systems can help achieve these objectives. In Chapter 16, "Preference" in the present volume, I return to the question of the objectives of the game-of-life, including further thoughts on the existence of multiple-prize lotteries discussed in Chapter 11, Note 3 (in Volume II). Each of these discussions takes the RDM or HDM preferences as given and considers how one should go about maximizing the expected value of the utility function implied by these decision-makers' preferences.

But, as we just saw, preferences themselves depend on "Society." Chapter 17 on "*Eudaimonia* for the Masses," later in this volume, asks how a "society"—including its political system, economic system, legal system, educational institutions and their curricula, and the moral standards that parents teach their children—should be "designed" so as to maximize "the greatest good for the greatest number" or other rules for "social choice."

FINANCIAL ECONOMIC DISCOVERIES

Hume's insights concerning statements about observable phenomena apply *a fortiori* to financial economics. Drop in on almost any financial economics seminar. There is a good chance that the lecturer will be presenting a paper that he or she hopes to publish—and perhaps thereby be one step closer to tenure; or is presenting it as part of his or her PhD dissertation. After a statement of the problem, the presentation continues with a literature review that ends with an explanation of why "last year's" econometric model on the subject was really not very good: because it failed to take into account certain variables which the presenter's research finds statistically significant, or did not have access to crucial data which the presenter has accessed by special arrangement, or did not use brand-new (or, in any case, highly sophisticated) econometric techniques now contained in the statistical package available at the presenter's school. It is not certain, of course, but I am willing to place a modest bet that "next year's" presenter's research will present an updated "prior literature," with an explanation of why the aforementioned research is to be considered obsolete.

This illustrates changes in belief due to changes in analysis, e.g., new data, new statistical techniques, new variables and/or new hypothesized functional forms. Such sources can cause change of belief even if there is no change in relevant financial relationships. But well-documented financial relationships—ones that individuals and institutions bet money on—can be (1) temporarily violated, or can (2) change "permanently," until they change again, permanently.

Examples of each follow:

1. "Black Monday," October 19, 1987, is an outstanding
   example of a short-term violation of a historical
   relationship. Based on historical returns going back
   to 1926, the daily standard deviation for a cap-
   weighted large-cap index was roughly 1.0%. On Black

Monday, large-cap stocks dropped about 25% on the day—a 25-sigma move! Previously, Markowitz and Usmen (1996a and 1996b) had concluded that the returns on the daily moves of the S&P 500 were not log-normal, as assumed in the Black-Scholes model, but log Student-t with between four and five degrees of freedom. Such a distribution has fatter tails than a log-normal distribution but, nevertheless, has only a negligible probability of generating a 25-sigma or greater move.

Examples such as Black Monday illustrate that just because some extreme outlier-event has *not* happened already does not prove it *cannot* happen; and those who place leveraged bets on the assumption that they cannot happen may or may not be fortunate enough to get away with it. Another example is the sudden demand for liquid as opposed to illiquid assets that wiped out Long-Term Capital Management. (See Rubin et al. 1999.)

2. Of the "permanent" changes in financial relationships, some have been reasonably predictable—with respect to ultimate direction, though not with respect to timing—while others were truly surprising and were predicted by few if any.

a. Financial fads that predictably end with a bang are ones in which funds are attracted because of the fad's performance, which, in turn, is due to the influx of funds to the fad, etc. Examples include the stock market boom of the 1920s, the high-tech bubble of the late 1990s, and earlier booms and busts as described in MacKay's (2013, 1841) *Extraordinary Popular Delusions and the Madness of Crowds*.

b. There seems to be a constant stream of exploitable "anomalies" that produce excess return on a risk-adjusted basis—until they attract too many followers. My own experience is that of running a convertible arbitrage fund circa 1970. (See Goodkin 2012.) Between 1970 and today the convertible arbitrage industry has grown substantially. To make a marketable profit, these funds now resort to leverage, which we did not need in 1970 or so. In general, Adam Smith's "invisible hand" pushes capital and entrepreneurs into investment methods that make above-average risk-adjusted returns—until they don't. This invisible hand is often clumsy, pushing too many entrepreneurs into a given kind of good or service—including investment services—until there are too many in the field, requiring a shakeout before the field stumbles toward a longer-run equilibrium.

c. I currently plan to devote Volume IV to work by various colleagues and me on how long do paradigms last and why do they change?

Probably the greatest "permanent" change in the world since the publication of Markowitz (1952)—unanticipated by everyone, or almost everyone—was the invention of the transistor. Thanks to Moore's Law (discussed in Chapter 12 in Volume II), transistors are a part of all sorts of "smart" devices such as, for example, your car, cell phone, and your many-featured modern oven. Transistor products facilitate the Internet, and therefore ecommerce. They are used by good guys and bad guys, and folks who just want to have fun. Who in 1952 could have predicted that people could someday avail themselves of MPT services via a pocket telephone?

Just because historical relationships change, or become temporarily breached, does not mean we should not look at history. But we need to remember that a good many investors (including some who considered themselves quite sophisticated) have lost a great deal of money, of their own and others, by assuming, with too great a certainty, that some historical relationship that held in the past as long as records have been kept would hold in the future, forever, without exception.

ECONOMIC ANALYSES THAT HAVE STOOD THE TEST OF TIME

We see then that markets change, and even when they change little, their explanations change. Nevertheless, there are economic analyses that have lasted a half century or longer—and are still going as strong as ever! What is different about these? The following three subsections of this section examine three examples, namely, the "law of supply and demand," the "Laffer curve," and mean-variance analysis.

(1) The Law of Supply and Demand

The so-called "law" of supply and demand is not a law. It is not even a hypothesis. It is a *model,* or a Platonic Ideal—like a Euclidean triangle. It postulates a situation in which two numbers are to be determined. Suggestive of the applications intended for the model, these numbers are named "price" and "quantity" and, accordingly, are abbreviated p and q. The model assumes that quantity demanded is a *decreasing* function of price, up to the price at which no one would want, or could afford, the good or service in question; and, conversely, the quantity supplied is an *increasing* function of the price, up to the point at which the maximum possible supply is brought to market. In brief:

$$q = D(p) \qquad\qquad (13.1a)$$
$$q = S(p) \qquad\qquad (13.1b)$$

where D represents the amount demanded as a function of price, and S represents the amount supplied as a function of price. (Sometimes one of these relationships is written with p on the left side and q on the right; but that makes no sense, since the quantities that buyers seek to buy, and sellers seek to sell, are functions of price, not vice versa.) It is assumed, for any particular application of this model, that the system of two equations in the two unknowns of Equation (13.1) has a unique solution—which is called the "market equilibrium," or "market clearing." If this equilibrium occurs in the region where D and S are strictly monotonic (decreasing and increasing, respectively), then the model predicts that the quantity offered will exceed the quantity sought if a flat price is set greater than the market equilibrium price; and, conversely, if it is set less than the market equilibrium price.

This model is neither right nor wrong. What *can* be right or wrong, for example, is the *hypothesis* that the long lines at gas pumps, when gas was price-controlled, were due to the government's override of the market—setting gas's price below the market-clearing price.

(2) The Laffer Curve

The Laffer curve consists of one equation in two unknowns:

$$r = R(t) \qquad\qquad (13.2a)$$

where R is the revenue function, t is "tax rate" as a fraction of income, and r is the revenue that the government collects at that tax rate. It is assumed that

$$R(0) = 0 \qquad\qquad (13.2b)$$
$$R(1) = 0 \qquad\qquad (13.2c)$$

In the case of Equation (13.2b), zero percent of any amount of GDP is zero. In the second case, it is assumed that if the government took all, no one would work. The government would get 100% of nothing. It is further assumed that R has a unique maximum at some $\hat{p} \in (0, 1)$ and that R is strictly increasing for

$$0 \leq p < \hat{p}$$

and strictly decreasing for

$$\hat{p} < p \leq 1.$$

In fact, perhaps R(1) is actually some small positive number with

$$r(\hat{p}) >> R(1) > 0. \tag{13.2d}$$

When a government taxes you, it uses part of its revenues to supply you with goods and services. These include, e.g., fire and police protection and street repair but may also include individual consumption items such as food stamps and medical care. In principal, communism takes 100% of your production and supplies you with what it thinks you need. In a city, it may "pay" you a salary, as compared to a collective farm, which takes all production and supplies all needs. But the salary is an illusion, since "the State" determines how much it is, and all production belongs to "the People."

As with the Law of Supply and Demand, the preceding is a model, not a hypothesis. The hypothesis is that Equation (13.2) describes the actual relationship between actual tax rates and government revenue. The general idea of the Laffer curve is believed by many (including me) to be obviously applicable in fact, and the first step toward fiscal responsibility.

(3) Mean-Variance Analysis

Mean-variance analysis (MVA) has become, and has remained, central to modern financial practice. For example, the Bank of New York Mellon (2014) surveys of institutional investors found that 74% of institutions surveyed used mathematical/computer-based analysis for risk-return analysis at the asset class level. An additional 18% used it from time to time. Thus, if the Bank of NY Mellon survey is at all reflective of the institutional investor population, all but roughly 8% of their tens of trillions of AUM (assets under management) are managed regularly, or from time to time, with the aid of MVA. In addition, it is widely used to advise individual investors, e.g., by GuidedChoice (GC), as described in Chapter 7 (in Volume II) and by 1st Global of Dallas, Texas, sponsor of this four-volume book.

I believe that there are two reasons for this wide acceptance. First, MVA is actually a minimalist approach to the problem of *portfolio selection*; and second, it is quite flexible.

As to MVA's minimalism: Surely large institutional investors, and individuals or couples saving for their retirement, want to avoid portfolio risk while seeking portfolio return, measured somehow. Avoiding portfolio risk must involve some notion of covariance, since everyone knows one should not put all one's eggs in one basket. The formula for portfolio variance, in terms of the variances and covariances of securities, makes *no* assumption about the *form* of the probability distribution. Many people are confused about this. Volume I of this book refers to this as "the Great Confusion," namely the confusion between the necessary and sufficient conditions for the applicability of MVA in practice. Normal (Gaussian) return distributions are a sufficient condition, but they are not necessary. My justification for the use of mean and variance—as presented in Part IV of my 1959 book—was *not* Gaussian return distributions but was the efficacy of mean-variance approximations to expected utility. Chapter 2 of the present book (in Volume I) surveys the extensive—and generally favorable—research on mean-variance approximation to expected utility.

Thus, MVA asks only for estimates of means, variances and covariances (or a factor model in lieu of covariances), and makes no assumption about the form of the joint return distribution. As noted in Chapter 2 (in Volume I), this may greatly simplify estimation requirements as compared to other joint distributions. As a consequence of its need for means, variances and covariances, or a risk-factor model, MVA serves to help organize an institution's thinking about risk and return on the portfolio as a whole.

As to MVA's flexibility, Markowitz (1959) presents the *critical line algorithm* for tracing out an MV efficient frontier subject to any system of linear *equality* and/or *inequality* constraints.[2] This is used in practice to put upper and lower bounds on the amount invested in any one security or asset class, on the total amounts invested in various combinations of securities or asset classes, on portfolio turnover, etc. These MVA inputs can be used to represent legal constraints, policy constraints, liquidity constraints and skepticism as to the accuracy of parameter estimates despite an organization's best estimates of parameters, given the time and resources available. GuidedChoice identifies a set of asset classes—including small-cap stocks, emerging-market stocks or bonds, and high-yield bonds—as Risky Sounding Stuff (RSS). They constrain the aggregate investment in RSS as a fraction of all equity investment, as well as placing upper bounds on individual RSS asset classes. The reason is that even if a larger allocation to RSS asset classes would be optimal to a young investor in the long run, any of these asset classes could take a big hit during a financial crisis, causing the investor to drop the program long before the "long run" arrives.

Thus, MVA is not a hypothesis, but a framework into which an analysis team can enter (1) their estimates of future security or asset class performance, including their comovement, and (2) their priors as to what are reasonable portfolios.

CONSTRUCTIVE SKEPTICISM

Recall that I recommend that everyone who seeks to produce or consume financial research do the Descartes exercise for themselves and heed Hume's injunction that past empirical relationships will not necessarily hold in the future. These are steps toward becoming a "constructive skeptic." By "financial research" I have in mind the proposing and testing of financial models, or other financial hypotheses, as opposed to research that ends in "buy," "hold," or "sell" recommendations (though the latter type of research could also benefit from a great deal of "constructive skepticism").

I speak of "skepticism" rather than "cynicism." Granted that there *are* kinds of research—those that feign objectivity but clearly are slanted to serve some marketing purpose—that *do* merit cynicism. This type of "research" is of no interest here—other than to warn the constructive skeptic to be on the lookout for such. For example, when presented with a copy of a PowerPoint presentation for some fund with a unique methodology, be sure to turn to the last page, with "Disclosures" in small print. Lawyers require money managers to confess to all kinds of sins there. In particular, if there are results that seem—in the body of the briefing—to be real-time, "live" results but in fact are backtests—then switch from skeptical to cynical. Backtesting is a legitimate research activity. But any omission or commission that might confuse a reasonably attentive viewer between real-time and simulated results exhibits a lack of candor and should count as at least two strikes against the vendor.

The goal of "*constructive* skepticism" is *not* to tear down and leave nothing (unless a whole line of research makes no sense), but to test the basis of a conclusion, like a quality control exercise, sometimes concluding that the researcher's data are biased (e.g., survivor bias in which only the firms that exist at the end as well as the start of some time-interval are included in an analysis), or that the method of inference from data to conclusion is faulty (the central subject in subsequent chapters), or that an alternative (not considered) hypothesis would supply a more plausible explanation of the data presented. Conversely, perhaps the conclusion is that the analysis holds up as well as could be hoped for in this world. In this case, the questioning process often produces additional insights as to the objectives, limitations and areas of applicability of the results.

It is important that not only the process be constructive in fact—but also that it is *perceived* as such. In particular, to be useful, the constructive skeptic must show no form of one-upmanship. The tone of the discussion must be one of equals seeking the truth.

I fancy myself to be a "constructive skeptic." This was not a reasoned choice: It just happened. As I noted earlier in this chapter, I began reading philosophers when I was in high school. Since I did not have to turn in a report on Descartes's Meditations by Thursday, I naturally thought long and hard about what I read—a practice that has served me well for the past seventy-plus years. In particular, if an author's position seemed fallacious—as it did when I read John Burr Williams (1997) or Friedman and Savage (1948)—I try to construct a better solution to problems they deal with, such as those reported in Markowitz (1952).

Finally, the constructive skeptic should, today, be as skeptical of the views they themselves held yesterday as he or she is of any other views. I hope I am, but that is not for me to judge.

In addition to being a constructive skeptic, I also view myself as being a *pragmatist* and a *Bayesian*. A later section of this chapter discusses pragmatism. Much of the remainder of this volume explores Bayesianism. I also fancy that I act according to "the scientific method" insofar as—or, in such manner as—it is applicable to financial research. But what **is** the so-called scientific method? Rather than try to define it, let us look at the methods used by unquestionably great scientists, such as Isaac Newton and Charles Darwin.

ISAAC NEWTON, PHILOSOPHER

Hume did not use gravity as an example of a widely believed empirical relationship, as I did in an earlier section. Instead, in Section IV of "The Connexon or Association of Ideas" on page 23 of his *Treatise on Human Understanding*, Hume tells us:

> A. *The qualities, from which this association arises, and by which the mind is after this manner conveyed from one idea to another, are three, viz. RESEMBLANCE, CONTIGUITY in time or place, and CAUSE and EFFECT.*
>
> B. *Of the three relations above-mentioned this of causation is the most extensive. Two objects may*

be considered as placed in this relation . . . when one is the cause of any of the actions or motions of the other.

In other words, FIRST the Cause, THEN the Effect.

Newton's "Philosophe Naturalis Principia Mathematica" ("Mathematical Principles of Natural Philosophy") (1966, 1687) was published 53 years before the publication of Hume's *Treatise* (2009, 1740). As Newton's model illustrates, often science predicts by relationships other than a simple first cause/then effect model. In particular, Newton's gravitational force works always and continuously. There is no before and after.

As to Newton's methods, objectives and basic principles, Newton states that he considers

chiefly those things which relate to gravity, levity, elastic force, the resistance of fluids, and the like forces, whether attractive or impulsive; and therefore I offer this work as the mathematical principles of philosophy, for the whole burden of philosophy seems to consist in this—from the phenomena of motions to investigate the forces of nature, and then from these forces to demonstrate the other phenomena; and to this end the general propositions in the First and Second Books are directed. In the Third Book I give an example of this in the explication of the System of the World; for by the propositions mathematically demonstrated in the former Books, in the Third I derive from the celestial phenomena the forces of gravity with which bodies tend to the sun and the several planets. Then from these forces, by other propositions which are also mathematical, I deduce the motions of the planets, the comets, the moon, and the sea. I wish we could derive the rest of the phenomena of Nature by the same kind of reasoning from mechanical principles, for I am induced by many reasons to suspect that they may all depend upon certain forces by which the particles of bodies, by some causes hitherto unknown, are either mutually impelled toward one another, and cohere in regular figures, or are repelled and recede from one another. These forces being unknown, philosophers have hitherto attempted the search of Nature in vain; but I hope the principles here laid down will afford some light either to this or some truer method of philosophy.

In their "Evolution of Physics: From Early Concepts to Relativity and Quanta," Einstein and Infeld (1938) date the modern scientific revolution to the works of Galileo and Newton. They speak of "The Book of Nature" as being like a "great mystery story."

Attempts to read the great mystery story are as old as human thought itself. Only a little over three hundred years ago, however, did scientists begin to understand the language of the story. Since that time, the age of Galileo and Newton, the reading has preceded rapidly.

I view things differently than both Newton and Einstein. I do not speak here of, e.g., Newton's laws of motion, the calculus, or optics; or Einstein on the photoelectric effect, Brownian motion, or general relativity. I speak rather of Newton's view that "I wish we could derive the rest of the phenomena of Nature by the same kind of reasoning from mechanical principles . . . " and of Einstein and Infeld's view that "modern" scientific methods and results in general, and modern physics in particular, date from Galileo and Newton. First, concerning Newton's view, I agree that the methodology used by Galileo and Newton has served the physical sciences well even as hypotheses have evolved (as Einstein and Infeld detail). But we should consider whether it needs to be amended, somehow, when applied to other fields, such as biology and financial economics. Second, I contend that scientific enquiry (by any reasonable definition of science), including mathematical models of the physical world, predates Galileo by thousands of years. I discuss my views on Newton in the following section and my views on the Einstein-Infeld quote in Chapter 15, starting in a section titled, "The Science Process."

FIELDS OTHER THAN PHYSICS

Not every observable phenomenon can be measured. Nor are the measurable attributes of some complex phenomenon necessarily its most important aspect. For example, Darwin took many measurements in his life as part of describing plants and animals of interest. But his world-changing *Origin of Species* is almost devoid of quantitative data or quantitative analysis other than the Malthus analysis of how fast populations would grow if not limited by their food supplies. The fact that this can be described by an exponential equation is not essential to Darwin's argument and does not appear in his book.

In his book *What Mad Pursuit: A Personal View of Scientific Discovery*, Francis Crick (1988) contrasts the methodologies of physics and biology. His background is physics. His fame is in biology, from his (and James Watson's) discovery of the double helix. Concerning physics versus biology, Crick tells us:

> [t]he basic laws of physics can usually be expressed in exact mathematical form, and they are probably the same throughout the universe. The "laws" of biology, by contrast, are often only broad generalizations, since they describe rather elaborate chemical mechanisms that natural selection has evolved over billions of years. . . . I myself knew very little biology, except in a rather general way, till I was over thirty, since my first degree was in physics. It took me a little time to adjust to the rather different way of thinking necessary in biology. It was almost as if one had to be born again.

Experimentation is not always possible. If one needs a total eclipse to test a theory, one calculates when and where one will occur and arranges to be there when it happens. If one seeks fossils, one digs. Even if experimentation is possible in a given field, it may not be the only—or even the best—form of observation for the phenomena in question. For example, chimpanzees are highly social animals. One can deprive infant chimps of the social contact that they instinctively crave and subject different ones of them to different conditions in a carefully controlled experiment. Perhaps this provides worthwhile knowledge, but it is certainly no substitute for Jane Goodall's (2000, 1986) carefully documented observations of chimpanzees in their natural habitat.

I argued at length in Chapter 7 (in Volume II) about why I think that asynchronous discrete event market simulators—based on agents who act according to observed or hypothesized investor behavior—would be a more useful type of stock market model than analytic models more akin to those of physics. More generally, as the title of the paper by Andrew Lo and Mark Mueller (2010) puts it, "Warning: Physics Envy May Be Hazardous to Your Wealth."

There is an important "deductive" process, which evolution has built into us, that requires "intuiting" (so to speak) the consequences of a given situation. For example, suppose that a smart, but overly reflective college student is called back from college because his father, the king, has died suddenly and his uncle has married his mother. Shortly after the student's return, he speaks with an apparition who claims to be the ghost of the recently deceased king and that his brother has caused him a painful as well as untimely death. What do you think would happen then? Specifically, suppose you had to write a play based on this situation *other* than Shakespeare's *Hamlet*. The process you would use to visualize the consequences of this situation would involve what I call *intuitive deduction*, in which you move from "premises" to "conclusions" by trying to "see"—and "feel"—the world from the point of view (POV) of each character with that character's strengths, weaknesses and motivation.

This is an example of the use of "intuitive deduction." We judge Shakespeare to be good at it because, given the postulated characters, the trajectory of the play seems inevitable. It is not, of course. For example, Polonius did not have to be hiding behind the drape in the queen's bedroom, or the gravedigger did not need to turn up "Poor Yorick's" skull. These events served to further the plot, and to motivate a sad philosophical soliloquy, "Poor Yorick, I knew him well."

You use intuitive deduction every day, for situations big and small. So did primitive man, and so do the predators and prey in the wild. They are reasonably successful in this, else their species would not survive. Intuitive deduction "thinks" through the consequences of "intuitive models," such as the setup of Hamlet or the mental "picture" of a car approaching from behind. Intuitive models themselves are shaped by experience, just as are formal models, and are just as subject to Hume's dictum as formal models.

Models may be "physical" rather than logical, mathematical, verbal or intuitive. Examples include maps, blueprints and detailed model ships. A road map describes a spatial layout. The assertion that a ten-year-old map, gathering dust in a garage, is still good enough for a particular purpose is a hypothesis that may or may not prove true. In the first instance, a blueprint is a directive; subsequently, it is a model of what could be true. The assertion that an object (e.g., a small sub-assembly or a large mansion) was actually built the way its blueprint directs is a hypothesis. There was a time when great ships were built from detailed physical models rather than from blueprints. The Maritime Museum, associated with the astronomical observatory in Greenwich, England, has a wonderful display of these models. As with a blueprint, in the first instance they were directives; now they could be hypotheses as to what long-gone ships looked like.

Financial practice draws on quantitative and nonquantitative observations and models. Since its principal objectives are quantitative, such as to provide a certain level of real consumption expenditures at retirement time, quantitative observations play a crucial role in modern financial practice. On the other hand, estimates (such as that of asset-class means, variances and covariances) should be forward-looking. These estimates may be based, in part, on what is currently going on in the world, e.g., what the Federal Reserve says about its interest rate intentions or political unrest in certain emerging markets. Estimates based on such "news" require intuitive deduction.

KARL POPPER

Popper (1963), page 517, says that

> a theory tells us the more about observable facts the
> more such facts it forbids—that is to say, the more
> observable facts are incompatible with it. We then
> can say that the empirical content of a theory is
> determined by (and equal to) the class of those obser-
> vational statements, or basic statements, which con-
> tradict the theory.

Thus, according to Popper, the "empirical content" of a theory
is the *assertion* that those phenomena whose occurrence would
cause us to *reject* the theory will, indeed, *not* occur. If no observation would cause us to reject a theory, then the theory has no
empirical content.

It seems to me that this rule works well for physics and
perhaps chemistry but is questionable for, e.g., biology or
financial economics. For example, what observation would
force one to reject the evolution hypothesis? I do not speak
here of Darwin's "natural selection" hypothesis, but of the more
fundamental hypothesis that one or more times in Earth's long
history, nonlife became life in some simple form; and all more
complex forms of life, such as many-celled organisms and even
eukaryote cells (with nuclei) as opposed to prokaryote cells
(without nuclei), are descendants of this original first cell (or
these original first cells). There are many gaps in our record
of life's family tree. But this is to be expected, considering the

short time man has been collecting fossils as compared to the countless species that exist or have existed—and the existence of species without hard parts, which therefore leave no fossils—our knowledge of the tree of life must necessarily consist of a few sprinkles of knowledge in a sea of ignorance. But if gaps cannot refute the evolution hypothesis, what can? I cannot conceive of any observation that would cause educated men and women generally to reject the evolution hypothesis.

An alternative hypothesis consistent with all observed— and foreseeable—evidence is that complex living beings were created—not all in a day or two—but from time to time over the course of billions of years. Once created, their offspring evolved by natural selection. Even though no observation can refute either one or the other of these theories, most educated people believe the evolution hypothesis rather than any alternative. This I believe is because the evolution-hypothesis, or the occasional-creation hypothesis, must take its place within a *system* of hypotheses—a *belief system*. Since any one individual's belief system contains an innumerable set of propositions on an enormous set of topics—from profound and universal to trivial and personal—it is possible that no two of Earth's billions of people have *identical* belief systems. But if we seek a current common core of beliefs among those who view themselves as "scientists," this core belief system has no room for special interventions from "outside" this world, at least after its Big-Bang start. The occasional-creation hypothesis just "doesn't fit."

Like the belief systems of individuals, this current core scientific (a.k.a. "rationalistic") belief system includes hypotheses that are believed with greater or less "certainty," hypotheses whose truth implies the truth of other hypotheses, and hypotheses whose truth is accepted today and will be rejected tomorrow. For example, before World War II, the notion that continents move was considered ridiculous. Now it is accepted as well established. When one part of any belief structure changes, other parts may need to be altered. In particular, hypotheses about how comparable species on different continents evolved take into account continental shifts.

One might conjecture that the scientific belief system is almost universally accepted by educated people. But it should be noted that there is a completely different kind of belief system to the scientific, held by many equally well-educated individuals—sometimes by the same individuals at different times—concerning which I can see no verifiable implication of either that would logically force me to reject the one or the other. I speak, of course, of the *mystical* view of the world.

MYSTICISM

In my Descartes-like exercise I mentioned the routine influences of religious leaders, e.g., one's minister, priest or rabbi. In contrast, I speak now of systems in which some are raised and others come to by either sudden, life-altering conversions to an organized religion or equally life-altering mystical experiences that transcend any specific organized religion.

William James, author of *The Principles of Psychology* (1980, 1890), and generally recognized as the "father of American psychology," writes about mystical conversions in his (1923, 1902) book, *The Varieties of Religious Experience*. The following is one of many examples of mystical conversion to an organized religion:

> *The most curious record of sudden conversion with which I am acquainted is that of M. Alphonse Ratisbonne, a free-thinking French Jew, to Catholicism, at Rome in 1842. In a letter to a clerical friend, written a few months later, the convert gives a palpitating account of the circumstances [page 223].*

James then gives an account of the circumstances that find Ratisbonne waiting for a friend at a small church in Rome. James quotes Ratisbonne thus:

> *Instead of waiting in the carriage, I entered the church myself to look at it. The church of San Andrea was poor, small, and empty; I believe that I found myself there almost alone.*
>
> . . .
>
> *[A]n entirely black dog which went trotting and turning before me as I mused. In an instant the dog had disappeared, the whole church had vanished, I no longer saw anything,*
>
> . . .

or more truly I saw, O my God, one thing alone. Heavens, how can I speak of it? Oh no! Human words cannot attain to expressing the inexpressible. And description, however sublime it might be, could be but a profanation of the unspeakable truth.

I was there prostrate on the ground, bathed in my tears with my heart beside itself, when M. B. called me back to life, I could not reply to the questions which followed from him one upon the other. . . .

In his Preface, dated March 1902, James explains that his book consists of a series of 20 lectures which he gave at the University of Edinburgh. Lectures IX and X are on "Conversions," with many examples such as the one just cited. Lectures XVI and XVII are on "Mysticism" with examples from Yogic, Buddhist, Sufi (Muslim) and Christian mystics. In Lecture III, on "The Reality of the Unseen," James tells us that

I spoke of the convincingness of these feelings of reality, and I must dwell a moment longer on that point. They are as convincing to those who have them as any direct sensible experiences can be, and they are, as a rule, much more convincing than results established by mere logic ever are. One may indeed be entirely without them; probably more than one of you here present is without them in any marked degree; but if you do have them, and have them at all strongly, the probability is that you cannot help regarding them as genuine perceptions of truth, as revelations of a kind of reality which no adverse argument, however unanswerable by you in words, can expel from your belief. The opinion opposed to mysticism in philosophy is sometimes spoken of as rationalism. Rationalism insists that all our beliefs ought ultimately to find for themselves articulate grounds. Such grounds, for rationalism, must consist of four things: (1) definitely stateable abstract principles; (2) definite facts of sensation; (3) definite hypotheses based on such facts; and (4) definite inferences logically drawn. Vague impressions of something indefinable have no place in the rationalistic system, which on its positive side is surely a splendid intellectual tendency, for not only are all our philosophies fruits of it, but physical science (among other good things) is its result.

Nevertheless, if we look on man's whole mental life as it exists, on the life of men that lies in them apart from their learning and science, and that they inwardly and privately follow, we have to confess that the part of it of which rationalism can give an account is relatively superficial. It is the part that has the prestige undoubtedly, for it has the loquacity, it can challenge you for proofs, and chop logic, and put you down with words. But it will fail to convince or convert you all the same, if your dumb intuitions are opposed to its conclusion. If you have intuitions at all, they come from a deeper level of your nature than the loquacious level which rationalism inhabits.

Earlier in the same lecture, James gives us this analogy concerning "The Reality of the Unseen":

The sentiment of reality can indeed attach itself so strongly to our object of belief that our whole life is polarized through and through, so to speak, by its sense of the existence of the thing believed in, and yet that thing, for purpose of definite description, can hardly be said to be present to our mind at all. It is as if a bar of iron, without touch or sight, with no representative faculty whatever, might nevertheless be strongly endowed with an inner capacity for magnetic feeling; and as if, through the various arousals of its magnetism by magnets coming and going in its neighborhood, it might be consciously determined to different attitudes and tendencies. Such a bar of iron could never give you an outward description of the agencies that had the power of stirring it so strongly; yet of their presence, and of their significance for its life, it would be intensely aware through every fiber of its being.

Another analogy would be that of a goose who feels compelled to fly with its flock, in a certain direction, at a certain time of year.

James's own work in psychology is rationalistic. His essay *The Varieties of Religious Experience* is also rationalistic in that it is mostly an account of an enormous number of observations of others whose own experiences strongly confirmed for them a mystical worldview.

In a previous section I spoke of *the* current scientific, or rationalistic, worldview. At first glance it might seem that, in contrast, there are *many* mystical worldviews depending on whether an organized religion is involved and, if so, which. But it must be part of the core belief of the mystic that all such superficial historically determined differences are irrelevant.

The belief system of the mystic must, to a certain extent, overlap that of the nonmystic, since the mystic and nonmystic alike eat, sleep, walk, talk (if permitted) and perhaps even manage the finances of a monastery. A book on rational investing must necessarily address the rationalistic *financial* goals of the scientific, the mystic, and those who "couldn't care less."

My own rationalistic belief system has one unanswered question concerning mysticism. Mysticism seems to be as old as mankind, existing from primitive societies to the present, and spread throughout the world. What was the Darwinian advantage for *Homo sapiens* to have a certain fraction of its population be mystics?

CAVEATS

Caveat one: The examples of mysticism and the occasional creationist hypotheses illustrate that Karl Popper's rejectability criteria cannot be applied universally *as is*. But I do not want the exceptions to overwhelm the principle: One must agree with Popper's views to this extent—that even though this is not always possible, nevertheless, given two hypotheses, one should routinely ask how their implications differ with respect to observable phenomena.

Caveat two: Two hypotheses may imply *exactly* the same *possible* observations, but not with equal *probability*. The implications of this caveat will pervade the remainder of this volume.

CHARLES PEIRCE

In his "The Essentials of Pragmatism," Peirce (1955a, 1907) tells us:

> *Now quite the most striking feature of the new theory was its recognition of an inseparable connection between rational cognition and rational purpose; and that consideration it was which determined the preference for the name pragmatism.*

I take Peirce's (1955c, 1908) "Pragmatism in Retrospect: A Last Formulation" as his final word on the subject. In it, Peirce describes its origins in the meetings of a small group of young men at Oxford, who called themselves "The Metaphysical Club" and who met sometimes in Peirce's study and sometimes in that of William James. According to Peirce:

Nicholas St. John Green was one of the most inter-
ested fellows, a skillful lawyer and a learned one,
a disciple of Jeremy Bentham. . . . [H]e often urged
the importance of applying Descartes's definition of
belief, as "that upon which a man is prepared to act."
From this definition, pragmatism is scarce more than
a corollary; so that I am disposed to think of him as
the grandfather of pragmatism.

In particular, Alexander Bain (2004, 1875), page 505,
tells us:

[i]s, or is not, Belief essentially related to Action, that
is, volition? I answer, It is. Preparedness to act upon
what we affirm is admitted on all hands to be the
sole, the genuine, and the unmistakable criterion of
belief. Columbus shewed his belief in the roundness of
the earth, and in the existence of an unbroken ocean
between Europe and the east coast of Asia, when he
undertook his voyages.

Bain rules out certain intuitive and stimulus-and-
response types of actions as indicative of belief. Specifically,
Bain tells us:

In the working of this primordial impulse, there is no
place for belief, any more than for deliberation, reso-
lution, or desire; the believing state is not yet evolved

or differentiated. It may be there, in the germ, but if all our actions were of this primitive type, there would never have been any mention of the state. Only when performing acts that do not afford immediate gratification, but are reckoned on as bringing gratification in the future, are we properly said to be manifesting our belief. The animal that makes a journey to a pool of water to relieve thirst believes that the object signalized by the visible appearance of water quenches thirst.

Bain's dictum, that my actions reveal beliefs, is illustrated by the example in my Descartes-like exercise of my driving under the assumption—i.e., in the belief—that there is no gaping sinkhole around the next corner. Another action I take for myself and recommend to others is to hold a diversified portfolio of securities. This reveals two beliefs of mine. It shows that I believe that I *do not know* which companies will succeed or fail, just as I do not know who did it in the middle of a detective story. It also reveals that I believe that the world economy, including securities' markets, will persist.

The problem I have with Bain's asserted relationship between belief and action is that I do not see how my concurrence with the Big Bang Theory will affect my game-of-life actions in any way. Nevertheless, in Chapter 15 I will confess to being forced to accepting Bain's doctrine without reservations or caveats. The reason is that while all empirical propositions can be doubted, not all should be doubted equally given available evidence. This raises the question of "degrees of beliefs." While, as already noted, my views on Bayesianism have shifted somewhat, these views are still based on what are desirable properties of rational *action*. Hence, whatever the pros and cons, my views in fact are in accord with Bains's dictum.

As to the fact that *my* acceptance of some current scientific thinking does not affect *my* action—that is irrelevant. What *is* relevant are the *actions* of specialists in the field in question. Such actions include the proposal, in speeches and publications, of hypotheses to explain phenomena; the public acceptance or rejection of these hypotheses by the other qualified specialists; and further work in the field by specialists (and aspiring specialists) assessing the hypothesis in question as correct. For example, it was as much a visible expression of intensely held beliefs for Einstein to write that he did not believe that God played dice as it was for Christopher Columbus to sail west in three small boats because he believed that the earth was round.

After his reference to Bain, Peirce goes on to say:

> . . . *A most pregnant principle, quite undeniably, will this "kernel of pragmatism" prove to be, that the whole meaning of an intellectual predicate is that certain kinds of events would happen, one in so often, in the course of experience, under certain kinds of existential conditions—provided it can be proved to be true. . . . Suffice it to say once more that pragmatism*

is, in itself, no doctrine of metaphysics, no attempt to determine any truth of things. It is merely a method of ascertaining the meanings of hard words and abstract concepts. All pragmatists of whatever stripe will cordially assent to the statement. As to the ulterior and indirect effects of practicing the pragmatistic method, that is quite another affair. . . . "By their fruits ye shall know them."

Beyond these two propositions, to which pragmatists assent nem. con., we find such slight discrepancies between the views of one and another declared adherent as are to be found in every healthy and vigorous school of thought in every department of inquiry.

Based on the preceding description of what is a pragmatist, I hereby declare myself to be one, with the caveat that for a theory to be "fruitful" (bear good fruits) does *not* necessarily require it to be of immediate material benefit to one or more persons. It may instead be useful in satisfying the need of many of us to know how things work, or at least to have an explanation consistent with the observed or reported phenomena.

Peirce's Pragmatism: The Fine Details

In the preceding section I quote Peirce as saying, "provided it can be proved to be true." The remainder of the paragraph containing that sentence and the first sentence of the following paragraph are

But how is this to be done in the teeth of Messrs.
Bradley, Taylor, and other high metaphysicians, on
the one hand, and the entire nominalistic nation,
with its Wundts, its Haeckels, its Karl Pearsons, and
many other regiments, in their divers uniforms, on
the other?

At this difficulty I have halted for weeks and
weeks.

Peirce's resolution to this problem, and my own approach,
differ radically. A couple of quotes will serve to illustrate how
our paths diverge, starting with the first sentence of the paragraph following the preceding quote.

The next moment of the argument for pragmatism is
the view that every thought is a sign.

. . .

The next point is still less novel: for not to men-
tion references to it by the Greek commentators upon
Aristotle, it was between six and seven centuries ago
that John of Salisbury spoke of it as "fere in omnium
ore celebre." It is the distinction, to use that author's
phrases, between that which is a term nominat—its
logical breadth—and that which is significant—its
logical depth. In the case of a proposition it is the
distinction between that which its subject denotes
and that which its predicate asserts. In the case of an
argument, it is the distinction between the state of

things in which its premises are true and the state of things which is defined by the truth of its conclusion.

. . .

For the proper significate outcome of a sign, I propose the name, the interpretant of the sign.

With the terms "sign," "significate" and "interpretant" thus defined, we come (after a while) to the first passage that clearly distinguishes Peirce's approach from mine.

Now the problem of what the "meaning" of an intellectual concept is can only be solved by the study of the interpretant, or proper significate effects, of signs. These we find to be of three general classes with some important subdivisions. The first proper significate effect of a sign is a feeling produced by it. There is almost always a feeling which we come to interpret as evidence that we comprehend the proper effect of the sign, although the foundation of truth in this is frequently very slight. This "emotional interpretant," as I call it, may amount to much more than that feeling of recognition; and in some cases, it is the only proper significate effect that the sign produces. Thus, the performance of a piece of concerted music is a sign. It conveys, and is intended to convey, the composer's musical ideas; but these usually consist merely in a series of feelings. If a sign produces any further proper significate effect, it will do so through the mediation of the emotional interpretant,

and such further effect will always involve an effort. I
call it the energetic interpretant.

Recall that "the question" at issue is how to prove that "certain kinds of events would happen, one in so often . . . under certain kinds of existential conditions." In other words, *the question* is how logical "induction" should proceed. Textual analysis is always risky, since Interpreter A and Interpreter B may both find an author's words unambiguous—but diverge 180 degrees as to what a passage's unambiguous meaning is. The outstanding example is the U.S. Supreme Court's often divided pronouncements as to whose interpretation of the words of James Madison et al. is correct. That said, *my* interpretation of the words "thought" and "feelings" in the quoted Peirce passages is that of an *HDM's* thoughts and feelings. Peirce is analyzing the process by which an HDM reaches a *conviction* rather than that by which an RDM would reach a logically necessary *conclusion*.

Feelings are not to be dismissed as intrinsically irrational. A basic question that pervades life is "Who do I trust?" From Charles Ponzi himself, creator of the eponymous Ponzi scheme, to Bernie Madoff, recent noted fraudster—and surely long before Ponzi and until this very moment—a great deal of wealth has been lost due to naïvely bad answers to the question, "Do I trust this person with my money?"—both in terms of the person's honesty and ability to manage it. Often (if not always) the "judgment" as to whether one trusts a specific person to do a simple or complex task depends on "feelings" or "intuition" rather than articulated thoughts to the effect that "I *observed* such and such; therefore I *conclude* so and so." The question of "Who do I trust?" is prehuman, and therefore its thought-process must be (in part at least) preverbal. Every animal—including but not confined to mammals—must constantly ask, "Is this thing friend, foe, food or mate?" A species like the dodo bird, that gets the answer wrong sufficiently often, will not survive.

The fact that a particular judgment is a nonverbal conviction based on informal observations does not make it either true or false. The feeling is, itself, an observation. The RDM who corresponds to a given HDM would duly note any favorable or unfavorable feelings that the HDM had with respect to a proposed money manager (or doctor, dentist, auto mechanic, etc.) and make an action-recommendation, taking into account such things as "objective" evidence, the frequency with which similar feelings by this individual prove right, and the utility that will result from two different types of errors, e.g., rejecting the manager when it can in fact deliver superior performance or accepting it when it cannot. Such choices must be made by citizens who sit on juries, directors who guide institutional portfolios, and heads of families playing the game-of-life. This typically involves intuitive as well as logical inference.

"One in So Often"

Charles Peirce raised the question of how "certain kinds of events would happen, . . . one in so often, . . . , under certain kinds of existential conditions." Mathematicians, philosophers and those who identify themselves as "statisticians" have addressed this question for centuries. Noteworthy contributors include Laplace, Gauss, Pearson (father and son), R. A. Fisher, Leonard J. Savage, hundreds whose work is reported in Kendall (1994), and many others. These contributors are traditionally divided into two camps: One develops or uses the now standard "objective" statistical procedures as developed by R. A. Fisher (1960), or Neyman and Pearson (1933), and their respective followers. These procedures are incorporated into user-friendly statistical packages that include the original tests, plus increasingly sophisticated tests based on the same basic principles. Thanks to these statistical packages, thousands (perhaps tens of thousands) of researchers per year can determine whether their data accept or reject their hypothesis—all without understanding the assumptions behind the procedure or its underlying philosophy. The alternative approaches are various flavors of "Bayesianism," as used by Laplace and Gauss, and championed by L. J. Savage. In Chapter 15, I present my reasons for being in the latter camp.

IMMANUEL KANT

Kant (1943, 1781) argued that spatial relationships of the real world, as revealed to us by Euclid, were products of our mind. For example, a released ball might conceivably go up rather than down, but it would do so in Euclidean space. A few decades after Kant published this view, the famous mathematician Bernhard Riemann (2007, 1854), writing as Riemann the philosopher rather than Riemann the mathematician, said:

> As is well known, geometry presupposes the concept of space, as well as assuming the basic principles for constructions in space. It gives only nominal definitions of these things, while their essential specifications appear in the form of axioms. The relationship between these presuppositions is left in the dark; we do not see whether any connection between them is even possible.
>
> From Euclid to Lagrange, the most famous of the modern reformers of geometry, this darkness has been dispelled neither by the mathematicians nor by the philosophers who have concerned themselves with it. This is undoubtedly because the general concept of multiple extended quantities, which includes spatial quantities, remains completely unexplored. I have therefore first set myself the task of constructing the concept of a multiply extended quantity from general notions of quantity. It will be shown that a multiply extended quantity is susceptible of various metric relations, so that space constitutes only a special case of a triply extended quantity. From this, however, it is a necessary consequence that the theorems of geometry cannot be deduced from general notions of quantity, but that those properties that distinguish space from

other conceivable triply extended quantities can only be deduced from experience. Thus arises the problem of seeking out the simplest data from which the metric relations of space can be determined, a problem that by its very nature is not completely determined, for there may be several systems of simple data that suffice to determine the metric relations of space: For the present purposes, the most important system is that laid down as a foundation of geometry by Euclid. These data are—like all data—not logically necessary, but only of empirical certainty. They are hypotheses; one can therefore investigate their likelihood, which is certainly very great within the bounds of observation, and afterward decide on the legitimacy of extending them beyond the bounds of observation, both in the direction of the immeasurably large, and in the direction of the immeasurably small.

Einstein said of Riemann (as cited by Pesic 2007, with further comments of his own):

"Only the genius of Riemann, solitary and uncomprehended, by the middle of the last century already broke through to a new conception of space, in which space was deprived of its rigidity and in which its power to take part in physical events was recognized as possible." Thus Albert Einstein paid homage to the man he considered his predecessor and inspiration in

shaping a geometric vision of physics. Few episodes in the history of ideas and science are as thought-provoking as the passage between Georg Friedrich Bernhard Riemann (1826–1866) and Albert Einstein (1885–1955).

Many years of tough mathematics by Riemann, other mathematicians, and Einstein himself intervened between Riemann's insight and Einstein's General Relativity (GR). If you think of GR as a giant intellectual edifice, built with techniques and results of many great mathematical minds, what Riemann's insight did was to clear the site of progress-inhibiting presumptions.

WHAT AN RDM CAN KNOW *A PRIORI*

Kant is a highly influential philosopher in the Platonic tradition, i.e., he believes that facts about the empirical world can be arrived at *a priori*, by "pure reason." In particular, as just noted, Kant believed that Euclid's laws of geometry are imposed by our minds and therefore could never be contradicted by experience. But, as Poincaré explained, the laws of physics and geometry are *joint hypotheses*, and Einstein found that the simplest combination of physics and geometry, needed to explain certain observable phenomena, assumes that space is curved in the vicinity of mass.

But if the laws of geometry are not empirically certain, what is? Is there anything we can know *a priori* about the physical world? I agree with Peirce that I cannot reset my mind to a point when I had no experience. But I can postulate a situation that will serve as well.

Suppose that the RDM family of the Ode were the descendants of an RDM exploratory community that had been flipped into this world thousands of years ago, like Captain Kirk and the spaceship *Enterprise* of *Star Trek*, to explore worlds that no RDM had explored before. It was now time for other explorers, from the now much-expanded RDM community located on Earth, to further explore other universes. However, unlike the *Enterprise*'s explorations of other galaxies, these other universes may be subject to completely different laws of physics. Automata, used to survey alternative possible universes, report that a particular "alternative universe" (AU) has intelligent life-forms in the sense that they are cognizant of a sequence of perceptions, and have thoughts; but since the laws of physics may be different, so may life. The question then is what constraints on possible observations are imposed by the fact that an entity thinks. In other words; it thinks, therefore *what*?

To take this closer to home, suppose that you and I have won the confidence of the RDM community, and we have been accepted as volunteers to go along in this exploration. We have been briefed as follows:

1. We will be "imbedded" into some thinking host without interfering with its own thought processes.

2. Our own thought processes will be the same as they
   are now, except for certain enhancements—specifically,

   a. Our minds will work like a very large set of parallel
      processors—as they do now, as described in
      Chapter 12 (in Volume II)—except that they will
      have supercomputer capabilities. In particular, any
      computation (such as a large simulation analysis)
      that can be programmed and is sure to run in finite
      time will be computed "in a timely manner." I.e.,
      our minds, while not infinitely fast, will be fast
      enough for all practical purposes given the pace of
      the AU.

   b. All known theorems in our CU (current universe)
      will be stored in your and my mind's database,
      together with a "fast enough" mental "browser" for
      accessing these.

   c. The answer to any logical question that can, with
      certainty, be settled in a finite number of steps is
      available to us: We need but ask. In other words,
      we will be able to do anything that can be done
      with "pure reason"—instantly, for all practical
      purposes.

3. As already noted, the "laws of physics," and all
   that goes into them or follows from them, can be
   quite different. In particular, the AU may or may
   not have spatial extension, and if it does have
   such spatial extension, it will not necessarily be
   three-dimensional.

a. As to how distinct beings could exist in a world without extension, think of listening to a monaural recording of a symphony orchestra. The human ear and brain can distinguish the horns from the strings, and the piccolo will pierce through even when the entire orchestra is playing tutti, fortissimo. These wave patterns all exist and can be distinguished. Analogously, we can imagine a "spaceless" monaural world with many distinguishable "sound bundles," like the sounds of each of the four different French horns of a symphony orchestra, or each of its violins, etc.

b. Conversely, if the AU is spread through space, this space could be finite dimensional or infinite dimensional, discrete or continuous, any of the strange spaces studied in topology (see, e.g., Kelley 1955), or none-of-the-above.

In our awareness of our own world, light, sound, odor, and physical pressure are forms of data-flow concerning the state of one or more parts of the world, transmitted to our consciousness via our senses. We perceive some forms of such data-flow and not others. For example, we *see* parts of the electromagnetic spectrum and not others. We do not experience the Earth's magnetic field as do compasses and some migratory birds. The AU may have less, or many more, forms of data-flows between parts of its universe than we do with ours. Some living things in the AU may perceive one subset of the different types of world data-flows, and others a different subset. The nature of these data-flows, e.g., how they propagate and what is their character, depends on whether the universe has extension and, more generally, how the state of the universe can be characterized.

4. Concerning life, all we are told is that life-forms exist and are of different "species." As to how these group into genera and such, anything that is possible is possible. We are also informed by the RDM's automata that living individuals begin (are "born" in some sense), live and die. Some forms think.

We, along with the other RDM explorers, will perceive what our host perceives, though we may attend to its perceptions differently than our host does. We do *not* control the actions of our host. We can advise it if we can learn the language in which it thinks—assuming it thinks linguistically like humans, rather than nonlinguistically like cats and dogs. The latter perhaps can be commanded, like dogs or coaxed cats.

A priori (before we have any experience in the AU) we can ask:

Q1. How should we go about learning the nature of the AU? and

Q2. Will our thought processes themselves necessarily impose some structure on our model of this world; and, if so, what is the nature of this structure?

These are the same questions that the original RDM explorers of our universe asked before they were flipped into it. There were certain conclusions that the RDMs reached before the flip—because answers to Q1 are true for any universe about which anything can be "learned" in any way, and answers to Q2 are true of any entity that can learn—be it (in our world) man, mouse, fish or robot (MMF/R).

Sensations

The RDM explorer knew that the universe into which it was about to be flipped would have sensations; or more precisely, the thinking entity into which it would be flipped (e.g., an MMF/R, as it turned out) would experience sensations; else there would be no world about which to learn or no way to learn about it. The sensations that the RDM explorer experienced in its host entity differed depending on whether the host was an MMF/R or other. If the host was human, then the sensory experiences that the host and the RDM encountered depended on whether the newborn human into which the RDM was flipped had all the usual human sensory capabilities or was deficient in one or more of these in some minor or major way, like being color-blind or being Helen Keller.

We usually speak of the human's five senses: sight, sound, smell, taste and touch. But there are many more kinds of sensations than in this conventional list. There are, for example, the sensations of hunger and thirst; the emotion to flee or fight; the sense of balance and the feeling of vertigo when the sense of balance is defective; and the senses of love, lust and compassion—sometimes simultaneously and sometimes not. There are senses that one would call instincts or compulsions, such as an infant's instinctive compulsion to suckle.

Similarly, the first thing that you, I and our RDM companions will need to do when we arrive in our host is to survey the available types of sense perception our host experiences. Or—to put it most succinctly, despite an unavoidable pun— the first thing we must do is conduct a "senses census."

Perceptions

One must distinguish between sensation and perception. For example, one may say that he or she saw a robin on the lawn today or heard a mockingbird sing. These statements make sense only if both the speaker and the listener have a mental model of what a robin looks like and what a mockingbird sounds like. Before a child can be told that it "is a robin" that is hopping on a lawn, it must be able to perceive (a) that there is a two-legged thing hopping on a lawn and (b) the sound pattern "ROB-IN." Perceiving an object bobbing in its visual field requires the child to realize that if he or she looks elsewhere and looks back, and there still is an object bobbing, though not in the very same place and not in the same orientation, that this is still the same object. As Peirce said:

> One . . . proposes that we should begin by observing "the first impressions of sense," forgetting that our very percepts are the results of cognitive elaboration.

An original RDM who was flipped into an earthly MMF/R found that its host had an uncanny ability to recognize what was the same object viewed again and what combinations of different senses went together (e.g., the sight of a bird and the sound of its voice). This was because natural selection, or a programmer, created our host that way. Our own host in our forthcoming AU presumably will have similar capabilities for its own environment.

Time

We are told that our host will have a *sequence* of thoughts. Thus, the AU may or may not have spatial extension, but it will have time. Our host may have a sense of the passage of time, as in our CU, even when an AU "clock" is not available.

Me and Not Me

An RDM flipped into an earthly host would have had to learn—along with its host, who might likely have an instinctive advantage in this—what, for its host, was "me" and what was "not me"—what that host could do with its *me* and what it could and could not do with *not me* stuff. The RDM also had to learn what its host wanted out of life and how this changed over time. This must be true of any world in which there is an entity that could use our council. If our host has no objectives, we cannot help it achieve them. If there is no clear distinction between me and not me by the host, who are we trying to help?

As to how we should go about the complex task of learning about the AU world, including our host's objectives and how to advise our host as to how to best meet its (probably ever-changing) goals: This is essentially the subject of the remainder of this book.

14

DEDUCTION FIRST PRINCIPLES

INTRODUCTION

Hume spoke of mathematics as "relationships among ideas." If he were still with us, we might ask him, "What ideas?" and "What kinds of relationships?" Here I present two examples of related ideas. The first was *not* the kind of ideas and relationships Hume had in mind; the second is.

In Act 2, Scene 2 of Shakespeare's *Romeo and Juliet*, Juliet speaks these famous lines:

> *O Romeo, Romeo, wherefore art thou Romeo?*
> *... What's in a name?*

The idea expressed before the ellipsis is related to that following it. This relationship must be puzzling if one assumes that the word "wherefore" meant "where" circa 1600. In fact, it meant "why" or "for what reason." Thus a twenty-first-century translation of this line would be "Why is it that you are named Romeo?" Juliet goes on to explain:

> *It's only your name that's my enemy. You'd still be yourself even if you stopped being a Montague. What's a Montague anyway? It isn't a hand, a foot, an arm, a face, or any other part of a man. Oh, be some other name! What does a name mean? The thing we call a rose would smell just as sweet if we called it by any other name.*

There are ideas here—including Romeo's name and a rose's smell—and they are connected, but not by formal deductive reasoning. The play's audience makes the connection immediately because of the context of Juliet's lines within the play.

In certain crowds the following Aristotle quote is as famous as the above by Shakespeare:

> *All men are mortal.*
> *Socrates is a man.*
> *Therefore, Socrates is mortal.*

In the notation of Gerhard Gentzen's "natural deduction" (see Horska 2014),

$$\frac{A \rightarrow B \quad A}{B} \tag{14.1}$$

Gentzen's version says that if it is already known, in some sense, that Proposition A implies Proposition B, and Proposition A is also known in the same sense, then one may infer that Proposition B is true in that sense. This is what I later refer to as Logical Expression (1).

Aristotle's version is not intended as information about Socrates. Rather, Socrates being human and being mortal are "placeholders" for propositions. It can be formalized in more than one way. One modern version would say that the set, H, of human objects is a subset of the set, M, of mortal objects. Therefore, $E \in H$ implies $E \in M$.

Another version is the one written in Gentzen's notation: The proposition "E is a man" implies the proposition "E is mortal." Therefore, if E is in fact a man, then E is also mortal. Just as Aristotle's syllogism was not intended primarily as information about Socrates, Logical Expression (1) is not literally about the letters A and B. These letters here "stand for" propositions, just as the letters "a" and "b" stand for real numbers in the following prescription for solving one linear equation in one unknown:

$$ax = b \quad \text{and} \quad a \neq 0 \qquad (14.2a)$$

which implies:

$$x = b/a \qquad (14.2b)$$

The propositions that are already known, "in some sense," are known either as *axioms, definitions,* or are *previously proved results.* The latter are variously called *theorems, lemmas,* or *corollaries* depending, ultimately, on the tastes and preferences of some author. The combination of the statements above the line in Logical Expression (1) plus the "conclusion" statement below the line typically constitutes a "step" in the "proof" of some proposition "to be proved." The conclusion of the last step of the proof is the proposition *which was to be proved,* **QED.** The proposition now becomes a member of the set of "previously proved" propositions.

This is the entire story of the "relations among ideas," except for a few details, such as

    A. What is an algorithm that a human or computer could follow that would determine whether a particular string of characters constitutes a proposition?

    B. What should be the "permitted steps" of logic—and therefore of math and *all* logical reasoning? I.e., what one or more kinds of propositions above the line in Logical Expression (1) should imply particular propositions below the line?

    C. In addition to these "permitted steps," what should be the "axioms of logic" themselves, also applicable to all deductions?

    D. Why don't authors of today's math books tell the reader what rule justifies each of the steps in a proof? And should they?

    E. What does all this have to do with Decision Support Systems (DSSs)?

F. What, finally, does this have to do with the great minds described in the previous chapter? And are there additional great minds that should be added to our list?

This chapter and the three that follow address these questions beginning, in the present chapter, with Questions B and C. These have led to heated, sometimes venomous, arguments about the foundations of mathematics. In particular, mainstream *modern* math—such as *measure theory*, including *probability theory* as a special case—uses assumptions and logical steps that some noted logicians in the late nineteenth and early twentieth centuries forbade—and some still do. As to questions A, D and E, I believe that

- There could and should be databases of propositions and their proofs, for logic itself, and for various branches of mathematics based on various logical systems;
- These logical and mathematical databases could be used by the novice to fill in missing steps in proofs, and missing justifications for steps; and could be used by experts to help answer a great variety of questions, which such experts do in fact ask, such as which axioms are actually required to derive a particular result within a particular deductive system;
- These databases should be both rigorous and readable; therefore, SIMSCRIPT M, as proposed in Chapter

13, extended as needed using its Level 7 facilities, would be more suitable than, e.g., PROLOG, as the underlying programming language for these interactive databases.

These math and logic databases would be "systems" in the sense of SIMSCRIPTs III and M and, as such, could include other systems as subsystems. For example, the calculus database would include the analytic geometry system as a subsystem and, therefore, in turn, would inherit the algebra and geometry systems that are included in the analytic geometry system, etc. Such logical and mathematical systems would be available for inclusion in the personal Decision Support Systems (DSSs) of mathematicians and scientists but need not be included in the personal DSSs of others. In particular, a database that covered Newton's laws and how these imply Kepler's laws of planetary motion, would include the calculus system as a subsystem and would therefore inherit all the systems that are included, directly or indirectly, in the calculus system. The Newtonian System database would be included, of course, as one of the subsystems of every physicist, but few subsystems for butchers, bakers or candlestick makers. Nor are they likely to be included in many of the wide variety of the decision support systems (DSSs), which were the principal subject of much of Volume II.

For over two thousand years the followers of Aristotle have debated the followers of Plato. It seems safe to predict that this debate will continue as long as civilization as-we-know-it exists. For over one hundred years the followers of Brouwer have debated the followers of Hilbert. Time will tell whether the Brouwer-Hilbert debate will be as enduring as the Plato-Aristotle debate. The remainder of this chapter relates

- How the Hilbert and Brouwer views were the culmination of a debate that started with Newton's and Leibnitz's infinitesimals.
- How Hilbert's (1971, 1899) *Foundations of Geometry* laid down the rules for rigor now followed by all branches of mathematics. Specifically, Hilbert (1971, 1899) showed how to do Euclid rigorously.
- Brouwer's objections to Hilbert's whole approach and the Great Debate that resulted.
- "Hilbert's Program," namely work by Hilbert and others, to rebuild logic itself according to the rules laid down in Hilbert (1971, 1899).

Subsequent chapters will cover

- Chapter 15: Gentzen's "natural deduction." Consistent with Hilbert's rules of course, this is the view I had arrived at independently, a century or so after Gentzen.
- Chapter 16: Abraham Robinson's "Infinitesimal Analysis," which I find indispensable in going from results I have proven for the finite-dimensional case in Markowitz (1959) and later to their generalizations in infinite-dimensional cases.

- Chapter 17: My proposal as to how to make rigorous math more accessible to the layperson, and perhaps facilitate foundational research in logic.

As to Question F, these three chapters will introduce a passel of great minds whom we have not met before.

THE GREAT DEBATE

Starting in the second half of the nineteenth century, the debate that had been simmering since the time of Newton and Leibnitz burst into a full boil. It was Cantor's quantum jump to understanding of the infinite that turned up the heat on the debate. The next few sections present a brief introduction to Cantor's methods and conclusions. Some familiarity with the basics of Cantor's set theory is essential for an understanding of

- The Great Debate circa 1900;
- The alternative viewpoints that a flexible computerized logic system must be prepared to accommodate; and
- Probability theory, beyond the finite sample spaces to which Volumes I and II are confined.

After this ever-so-brief crash-course on Cantor (101), we will pick up the story of the Great Debate with

1. Newton's defense against the criticisms of Bishop Berkeley and other members of the "British renaissance";

2. Weierstrass and Dedekind, who—to use a football analogy—moved the ball far enough downfield to permit Cantor's game-winning field goal; and

3. Kronecker. Except for mean personalities that made Weierstrass and Cantor each sicker than they would have been otherwise, the Great Debate would probably be between Kronecker and Weierstrass.

ONE MORE REASON FOR STUDYING CANTOR'S SET THEORY

There are two types of reasons to study Cantor, namely

- practical, and
- esthetic, almost mystical.

On the first point, our own most important use of set theory is as the basis of "measure theory," of which probability theory is a special case. See Halmos (1974). Concerning the second point, as well as the first, the Introduction to Erich Kamke (1950) consists of one long paragraph extolling the virtues of set theory, followed by a two-line paragraph concerning the contents of the book. The first paragraph of Kamke's Introduction, in its entirety, reads as follows:

The Theory of Sets, which was founded by Georg Cantor (1845–1918) and already developed by him into an admirable system, is one of the greatest

*creations of the human mind. In no other science is
such bold formation of concepts found, and only the
theory of numbers, perhaps, contains methods of
proof of comparable beauty. It is no wonder, then, that
everyone who studies the theory of sets is indescribably
fascinated by it. Over and above that, however, this
theory has become of the very greatest importance for
the whole of mathematics. It has enriched nearly every
part of mathematics and lent it a new appearance. It
has given rise to new branches of mathematics, or at
least first rendered possible their further development,
such as the theory of set of points, the theory of real
functions and topology. Finally, the theory of sets has
had particular influence on the investigation of the
foundations of mathematics, acting in this respect, as
well as through the generality of its concepts, as a con-
necting link between mathematics and philosophy.*

Religious allusions are not unknown in connection with
set theory. In particular, on the one hand, Kronecker is said
(by the mathematician H. Weber) to have said, "*God* made
the integers, all else is the work of man." On the other hand,
Hilbert equally famously said that "No one shall expel us from
the *paradise* that Cantor has created." Or, as first spoken by
Hilbert in his native German:

*Aus dem Paradies, das Cantor uns geschaffen, soll
uns niemand vertreiben können.*

The fecundity of Cantor's concepts is illustrated by the extent of the usage of "set theory" itself and its two major application areas: measure theory and topology. I have already mentioned that modern probability is a special case of the former field and will discuss it further in the next chapter.

The other area, topology, generalizes ideas such as "continuity" and "convergence to a limit." An example of the power of this generalization is that it provides us with a complete answer to questions concerning "under what assumptions" and "in what different ways" will a "sequence of probability distributions" converge to a limit distribution.

"VERY FEW UNDERSTOOD IT"

The first and arguably the greatest biography of Cantor and his work is that of the English mathematician P. E. B. Jourdain (see Cantor 1955), written three years before Cantor died in 1918 at the age of 72 and four years before Jourdain himself died at the age of 39 (of Friedreich's ataxia, an inherited disease that causes progressive nerve damage). As Jourdain said in the work's Preface:

> This volume contains a translation of the two very important memoirs of Georg Cantor on transfinite numbers, which appeared in . . . 1895 and 1897. . . .
> These memoirs are the final and logically purified statement of many of the most important results of the long series of memoirs begun by Cantor in 1870. It is, I think, necessary, if we are to appreciate the full

import of Cantor's work on transfinite numbers, to have thought through and to bear in mind Cantor's earlier researches on the theory of point-aggregates. It was in these researches that the need for the transfinite numbers first showed itself, and it is only by the study of these researches that the majority of us can annihilate the feeling of arbitrariness and even insecurity about the introduction of these numbers. Furthermore, it is also necessary to trace backwards, especially through Weierstrass, the course of those researches which led to Cantor's work. I have, then, prefixed an Introduction tracing the growth of parts of the theory of functions during the nineteenth century, and dealing, in some detail, with the fundamental work of Weierstrass and others, and with the work of Cantor from 1870 to 1895. . . .

The philosophical revolution brought about by Cantor's work was even greater, perhaps, than the mathematical one. With few exceptions, mathematicians joyfully accepted, built upon, scrutinized, and perfected the foundations of Cantor's undying theory; but very many philosophers combated it. This seems to have been because very few understood it. I hope that this book may help to make the subject better known to both philosophers and mathematicians.

The three men whose influence on modern pure mathematics—and indirectly modern logic and the

philosophy which abuts on it—is most marked are Karl
Weierstrass, Richard Dedekind, and Georg Cantor.

The biographical sketches of this chapter review the contributions of Weierstrass and Dedekind referred to by Jourdain and others who took part, on one side or the other, in the Great Debate.

FINITE CARDINAL ARITHMETIC

Cantor's "transfinite" arithmetic extends to nonfinite sets certain properties that we take for granted for finite sets. We start by reviewing these properties.

Cantor distinguishes between transfinite *cardinal numbers* and transfinite *ordinal numbers,* corresponding to the two uses we make of finite numbers. For example, we say that 10 people attended Johnny's birthday party, and Mary was the third to arrive. The number "10" is a *cardinal* number; "third" is an *ordinal* number. Cantor speaks of *transfinite* cardinal and ordinal *arithmetic,* analogous to finite cardinal and ordinal arithmetic. For example, if the party had 10 children supervised by 4 adults, then the party had 10 + 4 = 14 people present. If waiting Section A boards its 20 people before waiting Section B, and Mary Smith is fourth in Section B, then Mary will be the twenty-fourth person to board.

Cantor's definition of transfinite *cardinal* numbers is based on the following observation:

For finite sets, if two sets, S and T, have the same number of members—i.e., have the same "cardinality"—there exists a *one-to-one correspondence* between members of the one set, T/S, and members of the other set, T.

For example, if there are 10 cupcakes as well as 10 children at the party, each child gets a cupcake. No child is disappointed, and no cupcakes are left over.

Let us write S R T if set S_1 can be placed in a one-to-one correspondence with set S_2. R is an "equivalence relationship," since it has the following easily verified properties:

For any sets A, B and C,

$$A \, R \, A \qquad\qquad (14.3a)$$

$$\text{If } A \, R \, B, \text{ then } B \, R \, A \qquad\qquad (14.3b)$$

$$\text{If } A \, R \, B \text{ and } B \, R \, C, \text{ then } A \, R \, C \qquad\qquad (14.3c)$$

Cantor's cardinal arithmetic includes addition, multiplication and exponentiation, analogously to show how these arithmetic operations are defined for finite numbers. In particular, if we have two finite sets, S and T (e.g., the first with three jelly beans and the second with four jelly beans), then the "union" $S \cup T$—i.e., the set consisting of all objects in S *plus* all objects in T—has a cardinal number, n, that satisfies

$$n \, (S \cup T) = n(S) + n(T) \qquad\qquad (14.4a)$$

If we dump the three jelly beans and then the four jelly beans into an empty bowl, the bowl will then have seven jelly beans. It doesn't matter which order we dump the three versus the four jelly beans into the bowl, illustrating that (axiomatically)

$$n (S) + n(T) = n(T) + n(S) \qquad (14.4b)$$

Also, if we have three sets of jelly beans, the final count of beans in the bowl is independent of the order in which they are introduced, thus

$$\{n (S) + n (T)\} + n (U) \qquad (14.4c)$$
$$= n (S) + \{n (T) + n (U)\} \qquad (14.4d)$$

The number of objects in a set, T, that is the union of m sets, $S_1, S_2, \ldots, S_m$, each with n objects, is denoted as

$$p (T) = mn \qquad (14.5a)$$

If one arranges a tray with m columns of jelly beans, each with n beans in the column, and then rotates the tray 90 degrees, the rows become columns, columns become rows, and we *see* that

$$mn = nm \qquad (14.5b)$$

To similarly *see* that

$$m (n_1 + n_2) = mn_1 + mn_2 \qquad (14.5c)$$

one needs, e.g., m = 5 *pairs* of bowls with n_1 = 3 and n_2 = 4 in the two bowls of each pair. Equation (14.5c) says that it makes no difference whether one combines each pair first, getting m bowls with $n_1 + n_2$ jelly beans in each; and then dumps the m bowls into one big bowl, or dumps all the n_1 little bowls into one big bowl; then all the n_2 little bowls into another big bowl; and finally combines the two big bowls (with mn_1 in one and mn_2 in the other) into an even bigger bowl.

Next, suppose that we have a large supply of jelly beans of n different colors, e.g., red, blue, green, yellow, brown, black and purple. We also have a very large supply of baggies, which we fill with every possible subset of the n different colors, including a bag with nothing in it, plus baggies with

- A red jelly bean and nothing else;
- A red and a blue jelly bean and nothing else
  . . . ;
- A baggie with every color *except* red; and
- A baggie with every color.

There would be 2^n such baggies, since, if we number the colors 1 through n, some baggies have Color 1 and some do not; among those that do (or do not) have Color 1, some have (or do not) have Color 2. Among those that do (or do not) have Colors 1 and/or 2, there are those that do (or do not) have Color 3, etc. Thus, there are

$$2 \times 2 \times 2 \times \ldots 2 = 2^n \qquad (14.5d)$$

ways of selecting distinct subsets from a set, S, with n objects, including S itself and the empty set.

RELATIVE SIZES OF FINITE SETS

Questions of the relative sizes of a set itself (n), the union of two or more copies of the set (e.g., 2n) and the number of subsets of the set 2n are of central concern for Cantor's analysis of the cardinality of infinite sets. In particular, the reader can confirm that for finite sets,

$$2^n > n \qquad \text{for } n \geq 1 \qquad (14.6a)$$

$$2n > n \qquad \text{for } n \geq 1 \qquad (14.6b)$$

$$n_2 > n \qquad \text{for } n \geq 2 \qquad (14.6c)$$

$$2^n > 2n \qquad \text{for } n \geq 3 \qquad (14.6d)$$

$$n! > 2^n \qquad \text{for } n \geq 4 \qquad (14.6e)$$

FINITE ORDINAL ARITHMETIC

So far, we have dealt only with unordered sets—jelly beans of many colors, dumped into bowls in any higgledy-piggledy disorder. Let us now introduce order into the party.

The adults fill bags with one each of n different colors (e.g., n = 5, if then each bag would have, e.g., a red, a blue, a green, a purple and a black jelly bean). The children are invited to paste different sequences of the n colors onto cardboard backings. Such sequences would include

Red Blue Green Purple Black
Red Blue Green Black Purple
Red Blue Black Green Purple
etc.

The children are also invited to try to figure out how many different sequences can be made from n colors. The answer to the latter question is n! since there are n ways of choosing the first in a sequence, (n − 1) remaining ways of picking the second in the sequence, etc.

Let the letter L here represent the relationship "later in the sequence than"; i.e., for a given sequence S,

$$a \, L \, b$$

means that a comes later in the S-sequence than b. (This notation is temporary, since the relationship denoted "L" here because it relates to ordered sets of jelly beans, will be relabeled ">" because it relates to sets of "ordinal numbers.") Cantor said that two ordered sets, S_1 and S_2, are "similar" if there is a one-to-one correspondence, R, between the two sets such that, for any a and b,

IF $\qquad\qquad$ $a \, L \, b$

THEN $\qquad\qquad$ $R(a) \, L \, R(b)$

Here L is an equivalence relationship as defined in Equations (14.4a) and (14.4b).

In particular, two *finite* ordered sets of the same size, n, are similar to each other, since each is similar to the ordered set of natural numbers from 1 to n. This, plus the relationships among cardinal numbers summarized in Equations (14.7a) and (14.7b), implies the following: Let

$$T = S_1 \cup S_2 \qquad (14.7a)$$

represent the ordered set obtained by placing S_2 *after* S_1, so that all members of S_2 *follow* all members of S_1. Clearly,

$$S_1 \cup S_2 \quad \text{is similar to} \quad S_2 \cup S_1 \qquad (14.7b)$$

since both are similar to the sequence of the first $n(S_1) + n(S_2)$ positive integers.

The fact that relationship (14.7a) with (14.7b) is *not* generally true for *infinite* ordered sets forced Cantor to create a different "number system" for "transfinite" ordinal arithmetic from the one he did for cardinal arithmetic.

STANDARD ORDERED SETS (SOSs)

Before we discuss Cantor's transfinite cardinal and ordinal number systems, we should discuss the topic "what *is* a number system, anyway?" In particular, we have discussed the "cardinal numerals" 1, 2, 3, . . . and their ordinal counterparts 1st, 2nd, 3rd, ... Specifically, what are these funny marks on the page, namely "1," "2," "3"? For this we need the concept of a Standard Ordered Set (SOS).

An SOS is in fact what Cantor calls a "well-ordered set." I called it an SOS because SOS rolls off the tongue easier than SWOS. The purpose served by any SOS is the same as that served by a *standard length*. In particular, in the statement "there are three feet in a yard," the word "foot" "stands for," i.e., literally "stands in the place of," the length of the foot of King Henry I, who ruled England from 1100 to 1135," and the word "yard" stands for "the distance from Henry's nose to the tip of his extended fingers."

Today, the most widely used SOS is the Indo-Arabic numeral system, devised in India and transmitted to Europe by the Arabs. Many other number sequences have been created, and some are still in use, such as

- The binary, octal and hexadecimal number systems used by various computer systems;
- The Roman number system, carved in stone on many buildings; and
- Tallies such as

1 11 111 1111 ̅H̅H̅L̅ ̅H̅H̅L̅ 1 1111 11 . . .

The choice of SOS or standard sequence is a matter of custom and convenience, since the 7th symbol in the Indo-Arabic system is in the same position as the VIIth symbol in the Roman system and the ̅H̅H̅L̅ 11th symbol in the usual tally system.

The above standard sequences are all marks on paper (or papyrus, or in the sand, etc.). Standard sequences can also involve physical objects whose presence or absence, or whose state, defines the sequence. The abacus is an ancient example, as is the magnetic state of a sequence of magnetic "bits" in a computer memory device. The oldest systematic SOS is the set of "codon" sequences that constitute RNA (generally believed to have preceded DNA).

On page 62 of Georges Ifrah's beautifully illustrated book, *The Universal History of Numbers: From Prehistory to the Invention of the Computer* (2000), in a chapter titled, "How the Cro-Magnon Man Counted," Ifrah tells us that

> . . . the radius bone of a wolf, marked with 55 notches on two series of groups of five . . . was discovered by archaeologists in 1937, at Dolni Věstonice in Czechoslovakia, in sediments which have been dated as approximately 30,000 years old. The purpose of these notches remains mysterious, but this bone (whose markings are systematic, and not artistically motivated) is one of the most ancient arithmetic documents to have come down to us. It clearly demonstrates that at that time human beings were not only able to conceive number in the abstract sense, but also to represent number with respect to a base. For otherwise, why would the notches have been grouped in so regular a pattern [in groups of five], rather than in a simple unbroken series?

The advantage of a number system as opposed to marks on a bone is that eventually one runs out of bone-space but not out of numbers.

FINITE CARDINAL AND ORDINAL NUMBERS

Given a standard sequence of numerals, such as the Indo-Arabic number system, the horse in the third place of a horse race is in the same position—in that ordered set—as is the numeral 3 in the Indo-Arabic number system. Therefore, 3 (for third) is the Indo-Arabic symbol attached to the object in that—or any other—finite ordered set. A set is said to have a (cardinal) size "7" if its members can be placed in one-to-one correspondence with the Indo-Arabic signs up to and including "7."

All this is very familiar, of course, for *finite* sets.

CANTOR (101)

Galileo knew that there is a one-to-one correspondence between all positive integers and their squares; i.e.,

$$1 \leftrightarrow 1$$
$$2 \leftrightarrow 4$$
$$3 \leftrightarrow 9$$

and, in general, the number i on the left corresponds to i^2 on the right. Because of such cases, Galileo recommended that one confine size comparisons to finite sets. Cantor was the first to ignore Galileo's sage advice. Specifically, Cantor defined two sets to have the same "cardinality" if there is a one-to-one relationship between them.

Cantor also showed that there is a one-to-one correspondence between all positive integers, i, and all *pairs*, (j, k), of positive integers, as illustrated in Exhibit 14.1.

EXHIBIT 14.1 Examples of Groups: Weierstrass Definition of a Limit of a Sequence

$$a_1, a_2, a_3, \ldots, b$$
$$\text{Formally, } \lim_{i \to \infty} a_i = b$$

Verbal Definition

Let ϵ (epsilon) represent a real number for any positive value of ϵ (or, e.g., $\epsilon = .1$ or .01 or .001, etc.); there is a place N—in the sequence—depending on ϵ such that if $i > N$, then $|1a_i - b| < \epsilon$.

The rows and columns of the exhibit represent the first and second components of the (i, 2) pair. The entries are the integers k assigned to the pair in the one-to-one correspondence

$$k \leftrightarrow (i, j)$$

For example;

$$1 \leftrightarrow (1, 1)$$
$$2 \leftrightarrow (2, 1)$$

$$3 \leftrightarrow (1, 2)$$
$$4 \leftrightarrow (3, 1)$$
$$\text{etc.}$$

It is a corollary that there is a one-to-one correspondence between the positive integers and the rational numbers, obtained by viewing i and j as the numerator and denominator of the rational number i/j and by skipping over i/j rationals—such as 2/4—equal to fractions already—i.e., 1/2 in this case—to which an integer has already been assigned.

Cantor defined an infinite set to be "countable" if it can be put into one-to-one correspondence with the positive integers. Otherwise it is "uncountable." Thus, in particular, the rational numbers are countable. He also showed that there is *no* one-to-one correspondence between the set of positive integers and the set of all *real* numbers. This is a corollary of the following.

THEOREM

*The set of **all subsets** of a **countable** set is **uncountable**.*

Note that Cantor speaks of "cardinality" rather than "size," perhaps in recognition of the difference between properties of finite and infinite sets, essentially, when you add one more to a set. Specifically, if one adds one to a set of seven members, one gets one of size seven. One cannot put a set of size x in one-to-one correspondence with one of size eight. If one adds one to a countable set, one gets another countable set. One may *define* a set to have a larger "size" if the so-called smaller size set is a subset of the larger size set. But then the even integers would be odd ones. "Size" then would only *partially* order the sets of positive integers. Some would regard this property as incomparable. Thus, this device would not have solved the problem of restoring to the objects being compared the properties we expect for a particular "size" of sets. Dedekind, whom we will meet later when we review the two sides of the "civil war" among mathematicians circa 1900, defined a "finite set" as one that cannot be put in one-to-one correspondence with one of its subsets.

PROOF

Since there is a one-to-one correspondence between any countable set and the positive integers, we need only show that there is no one-to-one correspondence between the positive integers and the *set of subsets* of the integers. Suppose, hypothetically, that the following were such a correspondence between the natural numbers and the set of *all* subsets of such numbers:

$$1 \leftrightarrow a_{11} \, a_{12} \, a_{13} \cdots$$
$$2 \leftrightarrow a_{21} \, a_{22} \, a_{23} \cdots \qquad (14.8a)$$
$$3 \leftrightarrow a_{31} \, a_{32} \, a_{33} \cdots$$

where a_{23}, for example, indicates whether the number 3 is a member of the second subset in the list.

Specifically,

$a_{ij} = 1$ indicates that the number j is in the ith set

$a_{ij} = 0$ indicates that j is *not* in the ith set

Thus, a one-to-one correspondence between the positive integers and all subsets of such is equivalent to a one-to-one correspondence between the positive integers and all possible sequences of zero and one.

Now consider the sequence

$$b = b_1 \, b_2 \, b_3 \ldots$$

such that

$$b_i = 0 \text{ if } a_{ii} = 1$$
$$b_i = 1 \text{ if } a_{ii} = 0$$

(14.8b)

Then B cannot be the ith member of the list in List (14.8a) since it differs from it in its ith place. Thus, the hypothesis that there is a one-to-one correspondence between the positive integers and the set of all subsets of the positive integers or, equivalently, the set of all zero-one sequences is a contradiction. We conclude, therefore, that the set of all subsets of the integers is uncountable.

QED

The preceding is referred to as Cantor's "Diagonal" proof. It can be used to prove that if n is any cardinal number, then $2^n > n$; i.e., a set with 2^n members cannot be placed in one-to-one correspondence with ones with n members (that have subsets with cardinality n).

COROLLARY

The set of real numbers is uncountable.

PROOF

Let the sequences of zeros and ones in the preceding proof be a binary representation of numbers in the half-open interval (0, 1). Some real numbers have two binary representations; e.g., these two sequences

$$0.01111\ldots \qquad\qquad (14.9)$$

$$0.10000\ldots$$

must represent the same real number, since we assume—axiomatically—that there is a third real number, r_3, between any two different real numbers, r_1 and r_2. But it is easy to show (as an exercise for the reader) that

- There are only a countable number of Sequence Pairs (14.9), and

- If A is uncountable and B is countable, then the set C = A – B is uncountable,

where C is the set obtained by deleting the members of set B from the set A. Thus, the set of $r \in [0,1)$ is uncountable; therefore, the set R of all real numbers must be uncountable.

QED

TRANSFINITE CARDINAL NUMBERS

Cantor chose the symbol $\aleph_0$ (pronounced "aleph naught") as the cardinal numeral for countable sets and c as the cardinal numeral for sets that can be put into one-to-one correspondence with the real line R. The legitimacy of assigning numerals—a.k.a. cardinal numbers—such as $\aleph_0$ and c to sets that can be placed in one-to-one correspondence with the positive integers and the real numbers, respectively, depends on the easily shown fact that "can be placed in one-to-one relationship" is an equivalence relationship for infinite as well as finite sets.

THE CONTINUUM HYPOTHESIS

A problem that Cantor could not solve was whether there are any cardinal numbers between $\aleph_0$ and c. The conjecture that there are none; i.e., that c is the next larger cardinal after $\aleph_0$ or, as Cantor put it,

$$c = \aleph_0 \tag{14.10a}$$

is called the "continuum hypothesis." It was solved by Kurt Gödel (1931), who showed that no contradiction would be introduced into set theory—if none existed already—by assuming that the continuum hypothesis is *true*, and Paul Cohen (1966), who showed that none would be introduced if the continuum hypothesis is assumed to be *false*. In other words, the continuum hypothesis is "independent" of the other assumptions of set theory.

Since the continuum hypothesis is independent of the other usual (Zermelo, Fraenkel Choice [ZFC]) axioms, one may decide on the grounds of whether to assume it or not. Personally, I assume it. This way I have an orderly sequence of alephs. Specifically, $\aleph_0$ is larger than all finite numbers but not the successor of any of them. Then

$$\aleph_1 = 2^{\aleph_0}$$
$$\aleph_2 = 2^{\aleph_1} \tag{14.10b}$$

One may ask, "Are these cardinal numbers larger than any in this sequence?" The answer is that there is nothing in Cantor's implicit axioms or the generally accepted ZFC axioms that would limit cardinals to the alephs. The first cardinal larger than all the alephs is the *second* inaccessible aleph. Aleph naught $\aleph_0$ is the first, since it is not the successor of any of its finite cardinals which are at least as large as the second inaccessible cardinal and are referred to as "large cardinals," as compared to alephs such as

$$c = 2\aleph_0$$

which refer to the Akihiro Kanamori (2009) volume on large cardinals for further ascent into the numeric stratosphere.

TRANSFINITE CARDINAL ARITHMETIC

Divide the positive integers Z^+ into two subsets, *both* of which are countable, e.g., those which are squares, S, and those which are *not* squares, N. ("Z," as used here, is from the German word "Zahlen.") Since

$$Z^+ = N \cup S \qquad (14.11a)$$

we have an example of the union of two countable sets producing a countable set. Since "one-to-one correspondence" is an equivalence relationship, and the union of two countable sets is countable, Cantor concluded that

$$\aleph_0 + \aleph_0 = 2\aleph_0$$
$$= \aleph_0 \qquad (14.11b)$$

And, generally,

$$n\aleph_0 - \aleph_0 \qquad (14.11c)$$

for any finite n. The one-to-one correspondence, shown in Exhibit (14.1), between the positive integers and pairs of such, demonstrates that

$$\aleph_0^2 = \aleph_0 \qquad (14.11d)$$

whereas we have seen that

$$2^{\aleph_0} = c > \aleph_0 \qquad (14.11e)$$

LEMMA

Cantor also showed that

$$C = A + B$$
$$= B + A \qquad (14.11f)$$

where A and B each equal either $\aleph_0$ or a finite cardinal number.

The relationships in Equations (14.11a–f) show that transfinite *cardinal arithmetic* seems a bit strange if one knows only finite arithmetic. Transfinite ordinal arithmetic is even stranger.

TRANSFINITE ORDINAL NUMBERS

A set, S, is "simply ordered" by a relationship ">" if for every a, b and c in S,

$a \neq b$, then either $a > b$ or $b > a$ (i.e., no ties); and

if $a > b$ and $b > a$, then $a > e$ (i.e., > is transitive). (14.12)

In particular, both the set Z^+ of positive integers and the set R of real numbers are simply ordered.

Consider two simply ordered sets, S and T. Cantor defines S and T to be "similar," in symbols S ↔ T. If there is a one-to-one correspondence

$$f: S \leftrightarrow T \qquad (14.13a)$$

such that, for any two members, a and b, in S,

$$a > b \text{ if and only if } f(a) > f(b) \qquad (14.13b)$$

For example, the set of positive integers in their usual order

$$1, 2, 3, \ldots \qquad (14.14a)$$

is obviously similar to the set of nonnegative integers in their usual order

$$0, 1, 2, \ldots \qquad (14.14b)$$

Ordered Set (14.15b) is obtained from Ordered Set (14.15c) by affixing 0 before (14.15a). Now, following Cantor, let us affix an element, "ω," after Z^+, yielding

$$1, 2, 3, \ldots, \omega \qquad (14.15a)$$

Thus arranged

$$n < \omega \text{ for all } n \in Z^+ \qquad (14.15b)$$

Cantor defines a "well-ordered" set, S, to be a simply ordered set with two additional properties, A and B:

A. S has a least element; i.e., there is an

$$a \in S \quad \text{such that} \quad a < b \qquad (14.15c)$$

for all other $b \in S$ with $a \neq b$

B. Every subset of S that is "bounded above" has a least upperbound, i.e., **if** S contains *any* member, b, such that

$$b > a \qquad \text{for all } a \in T \qquad (14.16)$$

then T contains a *smallest* such element; i.e., there is a $\tilde{b}$ in T such that $\tilde{b} < b$ for all b that satisfy (14.17), and

$$b \geq a \text{ for all } a \in T. \qquad (14.17)$$

EXAMPLES OF WELL-ORDERED
AND *NOT* WELL-ORDERED SETS

1. The *real numbers*, R, are *not* well-ordered. For example,

$$S = (0, 1) \qquad\qquad (14.18a)$$
$$= (0 < r < 1)$$

has an upper bound. In fact, 1 is the least upper bound (LUB) of (0, 1). But

$$1(0, 1) \qquad\qquad (14.18b)$$

Therefore, R is not well-ordered, since the definition of "well-ordered" precludes any such possibility. Also, (0, 1) does not contain a smallest member, since 0 is not a member of (0, 1).

2. It is easily shown that any *finite* set of *real* numbers *is* well-ordered.

3. A *finite* set of *complex numbers*, $a + b_i$, is not well-ordered, but they "can be" well-ordered, e.g., by their absolute value, $a^2 + b^2$, and with ties broken by the size of a.

TRANSFINITE ORDINAL ARITHMETIC

A corollary of Equation (14.11b) is that for transfinite *cardinal* arithmetic,

$$1 + \aleph_0 = \aleph_0 + 1$$
$$= \aleph_0$$

and (Equation 14.15) shows that

$$\omega = 1 + \omega$$
$$< \omega + 1$$

Hence

$$1 + \omega \neq \omega + 1 \qquad (14.19)$$

More generally, Cantor (1955) shows that if A is any infinite well-ordered set and B is another well-ordered set, finite or infinite, then

$$B + A = A$$
$$< A + B \qquad (14.20)$$

All finite ordered sets of a given cardinal size are similar. Inequalities (14.19) and (14.20) show that this is not the case for transfinite well-ordered sets. Specifically, Cantor (1955) shows that given the cardinality of the set of all the different "not-similar" orderings for a set of cardinality, $\aleph_0$, "[t]he second transfinite cardinal number, $\aleph_1$, as previously noted, may or may not equal c, the cardinality of the real line R, depending on whether or not one accepts the continuum hypothesis.

EXTENDED SOSs

Previously, we discussed the use of SOSs (Standard Ordered Sets) to specify the position of a member of a finite set. Cantor's ordinal numbers, namely

$$1 \quad 2 \quad 3 \ldots$$
$$\omega + 1 \, \omega + 2 \ldots \qquad (14.21)$$
$$2\omega \, 2\omega + 1 \, 3\omega + 2 \ldots$$

do the same for identifying the position in finite or transfinite sets.

Cantor calls the ordinal number ω the first member of an ordered set that includes the sequence (14.15b) as its "initial segment." He continues to affix additional members to the Ordered Set (14.16), which he labels

$$\omega + 1, \omega + 2, \ldots, 2\omega$$
$$2\omega + 1, 2\omega + 2, \ldots, 3\omega \qquad (14.22)$$

The Ordered Sets in (14.15) and (14.16) are examples of what Cantor calls "well-ordered sets." The real line is simply ordered but not well-ordered.

Cantor *defines* a set, S, to be well-ordered by a relationship ">" **IF**

it is simply ordered by ">"
and has a first element, i.e., there is an a in S such that

$$a < b$$

for all b $\in$ S with b $\neq$ a;
and if T is a subset of S, formally

$$T \subset S$$

and there is a $\in$ S that is "larger" than all b $\in$ T:
a > b for all t $\in$ T,
then there is a *first* such b in S, i.e.,
there is a c in S such that

$$c < b$$

for all c $\in$ S, c $\neq$ b such that

$$b < a$$

for all a $\in$ T.

LEMMA

Every nonempty subset, T, of a well-ordered set, S, has a first member.

PROOF

If T contains the first element of S, then this must be the first element of T. Otherwise, the first element of T is the first element, b, that follows after the set T* such that

$$a \in T^* \qquad \text{implies that} \quad b < a \qquad \text{for all b}$$

THE PARADOXES (A.K.A. ANTIMONIES)

It turned out that if one is not careful in reasoning about infinite sets, one can fall into logical contradictions. In particular, the second volume of Gottlieb Frege's (1879) two-volume magnum opus, *Begriffsschrift,* which derives the rules of arithmetic from more basic rules of logic, was at the printers when Frege, a German, received a letter written in German from a British mathematician, Bertrand Russell (later, Sir Bertrand Russell), telling Frege that there was one aspect of Frege's work (already known to Russell) that had bothered him (Russell), and he could now show—clearly and indisputably—that Frege's great structure had a crack in its foundation. Russell's letter and Frege's response are reproduced in Jean van Heijenoort's (1967). Also reproduced here, from page 127 of the latter, is

Russell's response to Heijenoort's request for permission to publish the two letters.

Dear Professor van Heijenoort,

I should be most pleased if you would publish the correspondence between Frege and myself, and I am grateful to you for suggesting this. As I think about acts of integrity and grace, I realize that there is nothing in my knowledge to compare with Frege's dedication to truth. His entire life's work was on the verge of completion, much of his work had been ignored to the benefit of men infinitely less capable, his second volume was about to be published, and upon finding that his fundamental assumption was in error, he responded with intellectual pleasure clearly submerging any feelings of personal disappointment. It was almost superhuman and a telling indication of that of which men are capable if their dedication is to creative work and knowledge instead of cruder efforts to dominate and be known.

Yours sincerely,
Bertrand Russell

"Russell's paradox" was this: Frege permitted a set to belong to itself. Russell said to consider the set, D, of all sets that *do not* belong to themselves and to ask the question, "Does D belong to itself?" If it does, that means it does not, and vice versa. Russell's solution was to propose a "hierarchy of types," as described, e.g., in the introductory sections of Whitehead and Russell (1970, 1910). A proposition of one type could make assertions about lower types but not about propositions involving its own or higher types. In particular, it could not be *self-referential*; i.e., it could not make propositions about itself, such as: This statement is false.

This is an example of a verbal equivalent of the Russell paradox. Another is the following:

> Define a word to be "self-descriptive" if it describes itself. Otherwise it is "non-self-descriptive." For example, "short" is a short word, therefore it is self-descriptive; whereas "long" is not a long word, so it is non-self-descriptive.
>
> **Question**: Is "non-self-descriptive" self-descriptive or non-self-descriptive? You figure.

THREE DIRECTIONS

The situation of leading mathematicians at the beginning of the twentieth century, after the discovery of the Burali-Forti (1897) and Russell paradoxes, was like that of paleolithic man, who discovered that fire can cook food, keep predators at bay, and burn down forests. One solution to paleolithic man's problem could have been to ban fire; the other, the one adopted, was to try to carefully contain it. Eventually, man worked out completely different ways to accomplish the goals achieved by fire. In particular, except for recreation, advanced civilizations no longer warm themselves with flaming logs. We use other forms of energy—not only to warm ourselves and our caves or to cook and keep wild animals at bay, but also (for example) to move about, speak to friends thousands of miles away, remember appointments, do arithmetic, and magically transform the characteristics of the world about us, such as transforming a black liquid into a plastic pocket comb.

The debate that ensued over which path math should take involved prominent mathematicians on both sides of the debate, who had made notable contributions to various branches of mathematics. In support of Cantor's methods and results were Weierstrass, Dedekind and Hilbert, and those whom P. Jourdain described as

> . . . *mathematicians [who] joyfully accepted, built upon, scrutinized, and perfected the foundations of Cantor's undying theory . . .*

Against Cantor were Kronecker, Weyl, Poincaré and Brouwer. As previously noted, the Great Debate over Cantor's methods and results was, in fact, an intensified phase of a longer-running debate that started with Bishop Berkeley's attack and Newton's defense of the rigor of the latter's "fluxions."

What follows is a brief account of those who either supported or sought to refute Cantor's ideas, including what they were like personally as well as what their major mathematical contributions were. For the most part this information comes from the MacTutor biographies. For example, if you Google some mathematician, such as "Weierstrass" and select the link titled (e.g.) "Karl Weierstrass biography," you will get a brief account of when and where the mathematician was born, his parents, where he went to school for his elementary and more advanced education, his mathematical accomplishments, his personality, how he interacted with other mathematicians, including how he interacted with Cantor if he was contemporary with the latter, and how he died. Other sources of information about mathematicians' lives and work include the *Stanford Encyclopedia of Philosophy (SEP)* and Wikipedia.

FROM ARISTOTLE TO HUME TO HILBERT

The hub of Chapter 13 was Hume's rejection of Aristotle's *Posterior Analytics*. The Great Debate that we now relate concerns whether Aristotle's *Prior Analytics* applies when reasoning about the infinite and the infinitesimal.

The argument as to whether or not one needed to modify Aristotle's *Prior Analytics* started with Newton's and Leibnitz's use of "infinitesimals." Since Newton and Leibnitz did not have a formal definition of a limit—that had to wait for Weierstrass, centuries later—they could not provide a formal definition of, e.g., velocity as of some instant in time. Newton, in particular, needed an "excuse" to do the computations of the *differential* calculus that we now take for granted, such as (in Leibnitz notation)

$$\frac{dx^2}{dx} = 2cx$$

His defense of such calculations follows:

> *If, therefore, I should hereafter happen to consider quantities as made up of particles, or should treat little curved lines as straight, I do not wish to be understood as meaning indivisibilia, but evanescent divisibilia; not the sums and ratios of determinate parts, but always the limits of sums and ratios; and the force of such demonstrations always depends on the methods laid down in the preceding lemmas.*
>
> *It may be objected that there is no last proportion of evanescent quantities, because before the quantities have vanished the proportion is not last, while afterward it is nothing. But by the same argument one might argue that a body arriving and stopping at a certain location has no last velocity: for before the body arrives at the location its velocity is not last, while afterward it has none. And the reply is easy.*

The description by Newton that then follows can be modernized as follows: Suppose that one wants to measure the maximum velocity—dx/dt—that a particular car can achieve. This is to be done by measuring its speed (i.e., its velocity) after it has gone around a track a few times and then whizzes by a "finish line." Its instantaneous velocity is not its speed when it's approaching the finish line, nor its speed after it has passed the finish line, but, as estimated by linear interpolation, the speed *at* the finish line. This seems to me to make the intended concept clear, even though one could not yet *rigorously* deduce the familiar formulas from them.

Berkeley's argument against either Leibnitz's "calculus differentials," dx/dt, or Newton's fluxions, x, is that of G. Berkeley (1734, page 64).

> *In the calculus differentials, which method serves to all the same intents and ends with that of fluxions, our modern analysts are not content to consider only the differences, and the differences of the differences of the first differences. And so on ad infinitum. That is, they consider quantities infinitely less than the least discernible quantity; and others infinitely less than those infinitely small ones; and still others infinitely less than the preceding infinitesimals, and so on without end or limit. Insomuch that we are to admit an infinite succession of infinitesimals, each infinitely less than the foregoing, and infinitely greater than the following. As there are first, second, third, fourth, fifth, etc. fluxions, so there are differences, first, second, third, fourth, etc., in an infinite progression toward nothing, which you still approach and never arrive at. And (which is most strange) although you should take a million millions of these infinitesimals, each whereof is supposed infinitely greater than some*

other real magnitude, and add them to the least given
quantity, it shall never be the bigger. For this is one
of the modest postulates of our modern mathemati-
cians and is a corner stone or ground work of their
speculations.

. . .

Berkeley then proceeds to argue the absurdity of these notions. In retrospect we have to admit that they had no rigorous justification, but they reshaped the world and eventually found a firm theoretical foundation.

BRITISH EMPIRICISM VERSUS CONTINENTAL RATIONALISM

William Bragg Ewald's *From Kant to Hilbert* (1996) in two volumes is a priceless collection of mathematical works on the developments from the time that Newton and Leibnitz introduced infinitesimals. The one thing that puzzles me about the book is its title, *From Kant to Hilbert*, since

1. Its first entry is by Bishop Berkeley rather than Kant.
2. The whole fuss is about infinitesimals, and Kant's quote is clearly (as far as I can see) irrelevant to that discussion.

The reason for the large difference between what Berkeley said and what Kant said is that Berkeley was part of the British

Empiricism that started with Francis Bacon and John Locke and culminated with Adam Smith and David Hume. Kant, on the other hand, represents the culmination of the Continental Rationalism in which Descartes—and Kant himself—figure most prominently. These two philosophical sides of the English Channel continued the debate between Aristotle and Plato, the empiricist and the "idealist."

Francis Bacon, with his *Novum Organum*, came before Locke. But Bacon dogmatically rejected Aristotle's *Prior Analytics*, and equally dogmatically asserted Aristotle's *Posterior Analytics*, assuming it was his own creation; whereas Locke started the trains of thought that lead to Hume's great insight and a document that starts out

> *We, the People of the*
> *United States of America*

In retrospect, both sides (i.e., followers of Newton and Leibnitz on the one hand, and the British Empiricists on the other) were right. On the one hand, Newton and Leibnitz's methods and results were too busy extending and applying these results to worry about what Leibnitz's handy notion for a derivative, dy/dx, really meant. Even now most "applied" mathematicians, from rocket scientists who can calculate the trajectory of a projectile to the moon to those who teach calculus, don't know the Bolzano-Weierstrass definition of a limit—and couldn't care less.[1] Basically, the arguments on the two sides, then and now, boil down to this: One side says, *It may not be rigorous, but it works,* whereas the other side says, *It may work, but it's not rigorous.*

One side builds bridges; the other side perfected and used the rules of deduction. Newton created the model of the world that was universally believed until the start of the twentieth century, whereas those who sought rigor paved the way for the mathematics of general relativity, quantum mechanics, particle physics and string theory.

Karl Theodor Wilhelm Weierstrass (1815–1897)

I had the good fortune to take my calculus from the eminent mathematician Saunders Mac Lane. Early in the course, Professor Mac Lane told us that we were about to be taught the definition of the limit of a sequence, i.e., what precisely is meant by

$$a, a_2, a_3, \ldots \rightarrow b$$

or, more formally,

$$\lim_{i \to \infty} a_i = b$$

He said that some of us would understand it, and some of us would not. Those who understood the formal definition of a limit would understand calculus; the others would not. Since then, whenever I have had occasion to hire a mathematician, if the candidate seemed otherwise qualified, I would ask him or her what was the formal definition of a limit. If the candidate could not provide it, he or she was dropped from further consideration.

This standard definition is reproduced in Exhibit 14.1. It says that given *any* positive number, no matter how small—such as 10^{-1}, 10^{-2}, 10^{-3}, ... , 10^{-100}—there comes a place, i, in the sequence such that

$$|a_i - b_i| < \text{the given number} \qquad (14.23)$$

(The "given number" is usually represented by the Greek letter epsilon, ε.)

I never previously asked who first thus defined "limit." The answer, in fact, is Karl Weierstrass, who sought to proceed rigorously, as well as broadly and deeply, in his mathematical analysis. In general, MacTutor (1998b) tells us that

> *Weierstrass's successful lectures in mathematics attracted students from all over the world. The topics of his lectures included: the application of Fourier series and integrals to mathematical physics (1856/57), an introduction to the theory of analytic functions . . . the theory of elliptic function (his main research topic), and applications to problems in geometry and mechanics.*

> . . .

Through the years the courses developed and a number of versions have been published such as the notes by Wilhelm Killing made in 1868 and those by Adolf Hurwitz from 1878. Weierstrass's approach still dominates teaching analysis today, and this is clearly seen from the contents and style of these lectures, particularly the Introduction course. Its contents were: numbers, the function concept with Weierstrass's power series approach, continuity and differentiability, analytic continuation, points of singularity, analytic functions of several variables . . . and contour integrals.

. . .

The standard of rigor that Weierstrass set, defining (for example) irrational numbers as limits of convergent series, strongly affected the future of mathematics. In particular, MacTutor (1998b) tells us that his efforts are summed up in his biography in the *Encyclopedia Britannica* as follows:

Known as the father of modern analysis, Weierstrass devised tests for the convergence of series and contributed to the theory of periodic function, functions of real variables, elliptic function, Abelian functions, converging infinite products, and the calculus of variations. He also advanced the theory of bilinear and quadratic forms.

Unfortunately, Weierstrass's personal history is rather sad. His father, Wilhelm, wanted him to study law, finance and economics at the University of Born, in preparation for a career as a Prussian bureaucrat as did he, Karl's father. Continuing the MacTutor (1998b) account:

> *The result of the conflict which went on inside Weierstrass was that he did not attend either the mathematics lectures or the lectures of his planned course. He reacted to the conflict inside him by pretending that he did not care about his studies, and he spent four years of intensive fencing and drinking.*
>
> *. . . the conflict between duty and inclination led to physical and mental strain. He tried, in vain, to overcome his problems by participating in carefree student life. . . .*
>
> *. . .*
>
> *We described above the health problems that Weierstrass suffered from 1850 onward. Although he had achieved the positions that he had dreamed of, his health gave out in December 1861, when he collapsed completely. It took him about a year to recover sufficiently to lecture again and he was never to regain his health completely. From this time on he lectured sitting down while a student wrote on the blackboard for him. The attacks that he had suffered from 1850 stopped and were replaced by chest problems.*

Weierstrass was preceded by eminent mathematicians such as Carl Jacobi, Leonhard Euler, Augustin-Louis Cauchy and others, whose monumental output built much of mathematics as we know it today. But—insofar as continuity and convergence are concerned—none of them could have proved their results rigorously, since they did not possess a formal definition of either continuity or convergence.

Leopold Kronecker (1823–1891)

Kronecker's comments on Cantor's work were particularly stinging and personal. This was inevitable given Kronecker's mathematical beliefs and personality. As described in his MacTutor (1999a) biography:

> *In order to understand why relations began to deteriorate in the 1870s we need to examine Kronecker's mathematical contributions more closely. . . . Kronecker's primary contributions were in the theory of equations and higher algebra, with his major contributions in elliptic functions, the theory of algebraic equations, and the theory of algebraic numbers. However, the topics he studied were restricted by the fact that he believed in the reduction of all mathematics to arguments involving only the integers and a finite number of steps. Kronecker is well known for his remark: "God created the integers, all else is the work of man. . . ." He was the first to doubt*

the significance of nonconstructive existence proofs. It appears that, from the early 1870s, Kronecker was opposed to the use of irrational numbers, upper and lower limits, and the Bolzano-Weierstrass theorem, because of their nonconstructive nature.

(The "Bolzano" just mentioned was Bernard Bolzano [1781–1848], born 34 years before Weierstrass. Bolzano surely would have been called the father of modern analysis instead of Weierstrass if more of his massive notebooks had been published in a timely manner.[2] See Bolzano's MacTutor [2005a] biography for details.)

Continuing with Kronecker:

Although Kronecker's view of mathematics was well known to his colleagues throughout the 1870s and 1880s, it was not until 1886 that he made these views public. In that year he argued against the theory of irrational numbers used by Dedekind, Cantor and Eduard Heine.

. . .

Another feature of Kronecker's personality was that he tended to fall out personally with those whom he disagreed with mathematically. Of course, given his belief that only finitely constructible mathematical objects existed, he was completely opposed to Cantor's developing ideas in set theory. Not only was Dedekind's, Heine's and Cantor's mathematics unacceptable to this way of thinking, but Weierstrass also came to feel that Kronecker was trying to convince the next generation of mathematicians that Weierstrass's work on analysis was of no value.

. . .

By 1888 Weierstrass felt that he could no longer work with Kronecker in Berlin and decided to go to Switzerland, but then, realizing that Kronecker would be in a strong position to influence the choice of his successor, he decided to remain in Berlin.

. . .

From time to time Cantor was depressed. It has been often conjectured that his depressions were caused by his failure to resolve the truth or falsity of the "continuum hypothesis, or by Kronecker's insults, or both. It is now believed that Cantor was bipolar, but the situation with the continuum hypothesis and Kronecker certainly did not help.

WHO CREATED WHAT?

In the beginning—not the genesis of the world, but when animals became aware of their environment—they found that, as far as they could see, of all possible worlds there were this one-dimensional *time*, three-dimensional *space*, and *things*. Among things, there were those that could eat you, those that you could eat, and things that you could stub a toe on. Depending on their life-span, all sentient creatures had to come to terms with day and night, summer and winter, birth, youth, old age and death. They had to move from one place to another. In particular, they had to understand "velocity"— how fast they moved as compared to things they wanted to eat or things that wanted to eat them.

By 30,000 years ago, *man* had *created the integers*. By the dawn of history—when writing came into existence—the Egyptians understood geometry well enough to build pyramids. Circa 600 BC, Thales invented the concept of "Proof." Circa 500 BC, the Pythagoreans discovered that (in modern garb)

$$c^2 = a^2 + b^2 \qquad (14.24)$$

where c is the length of the hypothenuse of a right triangle, and a and b are the lengths of the other two sides. In particular, if

$$a = b = 1 \qquad (14.25)$$

then

$$c = \sqrt{2} \qquad (14.26)$$

which the Pythagoreans were horrified to discover was not the ratio of two integers. They said such a number is *crazy*! Or, in Greek, "irrational."

One of the miracles of ancient Greece was Euclid's *Elements*, a thirteen-volume systematic account of mathematics at the time, including facts about numbers, such as that every integer is a product of primes, unique except for order, and facts about two- and three-dimensional space, such as how to bisect a line interval with straight edge and compass. Thus, man could create two intervals equal to half a given length and, by repeating this construction, four intervals that were each one-fourth the given interval, or eight such intervals, etc. By marking off, e.g., three adjacent such intervals, one could get an interval 3/8ths a given length, etc. While one cannot trisect an angle with straight edge and compass, one can visualize and define a segment divided into three equal segments and, from these, two adjacent segments taken together. In the same manner one can visualize and define, if not construct with compass and straight edge, any rational portion of an arbitrarily marked off unit segment.

Conclusion: God created time, space and things, whereas man created whatever he or she needed to understand such stuff.

Julius Wilhelm Richard Dedekind (1831–1916)

Richard Dedekind was 14 years older than Cantor. He and Riemann had been students together at Göttingen. According to his MacTutor (1998a) biography, Dedekind took a course on least squares estimation from Carl Friedrich Gauss.

> *. . . fifty years later Dedekind remembered the lectures as the most beautiful he had ever heard, writing that*

he had followed Gauss with constantly increasing
interest and that he could not forget the experience.

Dedekind's mostly widely known contribution to the foundation of mathematics is the "Dedekind Cut" of 1872. The issue he addressed was how to *define* a set of mathematical objects that had all the properties one ascribes to the real numbers. Such sets of objects had already been long known, and taken for granted, for the integers and rationals, namely any Standard Ordered Sequence (SOS) as an example of a set of objects with all the attributes one ascribes to "The Integers" and the ratios of such as the well-known representation of the portions of a pie one can take if one divides the pie in n equal parts and then gathers together m of them.

We saw that Weierstrass had defined real numbers in terms of some kind of convergent series. But that used nineteenth-century mathematics to define an ancient Greek concept. The proper "geometric" definition of an irrational number should have made sense to the Pythagoreans while, nevertheless, meeting modern standards of rigor.

Dedekind's solution to this is simplicity itself. It is analogous in a certain way to a Euclidean construction, in that Euclid said that given this and that, a new kind of object can be constructed. Similarly, Dedekind said, in effect, that the concepts of "rational number," "greater than" and "set" are well-defined. From these I will define *any* number, rational or irrational.

What is the number $\sqrt{2}$? How would you describe it? How can that be used as a formal definition of a set of objects that have all the properties that we ascribe to the "real numbers," including both rational and irrational.

Imagine the set of all rational numbers arrayed from left to right. "Cut" this array into two sets, S_L and S_U, such that

$$X^2 \geq 2 \text{ for all } x \in S_U$$
$$X^2 < 2 \text{ for all } x \in S_L \qquad (14.2)$$

This is Dedekind's definition of $\sqrt{2}$. We know it is irrational because $x \notin S_U$. The set of all such "cuts" is the set of real numbers. More precisely, they constitute a set of well-defined mathematical objects with all the properties we ascribe to the real numbers.

According to MacTutor (1998a), Dedekind met Cantor in 1874 when both were vacationing in the same area. Dedekind was sympathetic to Cantor's set theory, as is illustrated by the following quote from Dedekind's monograph, "Was sind und was sollen die Zahlen," penned 14 years after the Dedekind-Cantor meeting. With regard to determining whether a given element belongs to a given set:

> [i]n what way the determination comes about, or whether we know a way to decide it, is a matter of no consequence in what follows. The general laws that are to be developed do not depend on this at all.

In this quote Dedekind is arguing against Kronecker's objections to Cantor's assumptions, methods and results.

David Hilbert (1862–1943)

The keystone in the development of rigorous math, including the then "new math" of Newton and Leibowitz, was Hilbert's (1971, 1899) *The Foundations of Geometry*. The following year, 1900, the beginning of the *new* century, Hilbert published 23 Problems for the mathematicians of the twentieth century to solve. Exhibit 14.2 is a copy of a Wikipedia (2019a) table on the current (2019) status of Hilbert's problems. Some have been solved or shown to be unsolvable. Others are still open. Thus Hilbert's (1971, 1899) book was the last word in the nineteenth-century search for rigor, and his 23 Problems set the initial agenda for the twentieth century's ever-expanding quest to build on the foundations pioneered by Weierstrass, Dedekind, Cantor and Hilbert.

EXHIBIT 14.2 Hilbert's 23 Mathematical Problems

1. Cantor's problem of the cardinal number of the continuum
2. The compatibility of the arithmetic axioms
3. The equality of two volumes of two tetrahedra of equal bases and equal altitudes
4. The problem of the straight line as the shortest distance between two points
5. Lie's concept of a continuous group of transformations without the assumption of the differentiability of the functions defining the group (i.e., are continuous groups automatically differential groups?)
6. Mathematical treatment of the axioms of physics
7. Irrationality and transcendence of certain numbers
8. Problems (with the distribution) of prime numbers

9. Proof of the most general law of reciprocity in any number field
10. Determination of the solvability of a Diophantine equation
11. Quadratic forms with any algebraic numerical
12. Extension of Kronecker's theorem on abelian fields
13. Impossibility of the solution of the general equation of the seventh degree
14. Proof of the finiteness of certain complete systems of function
15. Rigorous foundation of Schubert's calculus
16. Problem of the topology of algebraic curves and surfaces
17. Express of definite forms by squares
18. Building space from congruent polys 23 hedra
19. Are the solutions of regular problems in the calculus of variations always necessarily analytic?
20. The general problem of boundary curves
21. Proof of the existence of linear differential equations having a prescribed monodromic group
22. Uniformization of analytic relations by means of automorphic functions
23. Further development of the methods of the calculus of variations

MacTutor (2014) describes Hilbert's extensive travels early in his career to learn from the great mathematicians of the day. One of Hilbert's professors suggested he visit Felix Klein in Leipzig.

Taking this advice, he went to Leipzig and attended Klein's lectures. He also got to know Georg Pick and Eduard Study. Klein suggested that both Hilbert and

Study should visit Erlangen and discuss their research with Paul Gordan, who was the leading expert on invariant theory. However, the visit did not take place at that time. Klein then told both Study and Hilbert that they should visit Paris. They both went in early 1886, Hilbert at the end of March. Klein had given them instructions as to which of the Paris mathematicians they should visit and they did as he told them, alternately writing to Klein about their experiences. One of the first mathematicians they visited was Henri Poincaré, who returned their visit a few days later.

. . .

In Paris, Camille Jordan gave a dinner for Hilbert and Study to which George-Henri Halphen, Amédéé Mannheim and Gaston Darboux were invited. On this occasion the French mathematicians all spoke German out of politeness to their German guests, who complained to Klein afterward that the mathematical conversation had been very superficial.

. . .

The mathematician with whom they seemed to get on best was Charles Hermite. Although they considered him very old (he was 64), he was "extraordinarily friendly and hospitable" and discussed the big problems of invariant theory. Since they had found their visit especially useful, they returned to Hermite's home for a second visit a few days later. It is clear that Hilbert's thoughts were entirely on mathematics

*during his time in Paris and he wrote nothing of any
sightseeing.*

. . .

*. . . [H]e {Hilbert] set off in March 1888 on a tour
of several leading mathematical centers in Germany,
including Berlin, Leipzig, and Göttingen. During the
course of a month, he spoke with some 20 mathematicians from whom he gained a stimulating overview
of current research interests throughout the country.*

. . .

*In Berlin he met Kronecker and Weierstrass,
who presented the young Hilbert with two rather different views of the future. Next, in Leipzig, he finally
met Paul Gordan.*

*. . . [T]he two hit it off splendidly, as both loved
nothing more than to talk about mathematics.*

His MacTutor (2014) article describes several fields
in which Hilbert made contributions. In particular, it notes
that "today Hilbert's name is often best remembered through
the concept of a Hilbert space." It goes on to quote Irving
Kaplansky on the origins of this concept.

*Hilbert's work in integral equations in about 1909 led
directly to twentieth-century research in functional
analysis (the branch of mathematics in which functions are studied collectively). This work also established the basis for his work on infinite-dimensional*

space, later called Hilbert space, a concept that is use-
ful in mathematical analysis and quantum mechanics.
Making use of his results on integral equations, Hilbert
contributed to the development of mathematical phys-
ics by his important memoirs on kinetic gas theory and
the theory of radiations.

MacTutor (2014) cites Otto Blumenthal on Hilbert's mathematical abilities.

In the analysis of mathematical talent, one has to dif-
ferentiate between the ability to create new concepts
that generate new types of thought structures and
the gift for sensing deeper connections and under-
lying unity. In Hilbert's case, his greatness lies in an
immensely powerful insight that penetrates into the
depths of a question. All of his works contain exam-
ples from far-flung fields in which only he was able to
discern an interrelatedness and connection with the
problem at hand. From these, the synthesis, his work
of art, was ultimately created. Insofar as the creation
of new ideas is concerned, I would place [Hermann]
Minkowski higher, and of the classical great ones, [Carl
Friedrich] Gauss, [Évariste] Galois, and Riemann. But
when it comes to penetrating insight, only a few of the
very greatest were the equal of Hilbert.

MacTutor (2014) also tells us that "[a]mong Hilbert's students were Hermann Weyl, the famous world chess champion Emmanuel Lasker, and Ernst Zermelo. But the list includes many other famous names including . . . and a list of nineteen names follows. Among Hilbert's students were Hermann Weyl, the famous world chess champion Emanuel Lasker, and Ernst Zermelo. But the list includes many other famous names including Wilhelm Ackermann, Felix Bernstein, Otto Blumenthal, Richard Courant, Haskell Curry, Max Dehn, Rudolf Fueter, Alfred Haar, Georg Hamel, Erich Hecke, Earle Hedrick, Ernst Hellinger, Edward Kasner, Oliver Kellogg, Hellmuth Kneser, Otto Neugebauer, Erhard Schmidt, Hugo Steinhaus, and Teiji Takagi. The only name on the list that is included in my personal library is Richard Courant. In particular, I have copies of Courant's *Calculus*, Volumes I and II, at my offices (a) at my home, (b) at the Harry Markowitz Company, and (c) at Guided Choice. My library at the Harry Markowitz Company also includes Hilbert and Courant's *Mathematical Physics*. Courant explains that he wrote this book's two volumes, but the ideas were Hilbert's. Finally, my library also includes works by one of Hilbert's students who didn't make MacTutor's list, namely John von Neumann.

Continuing with Hilbert's biography,

> . . . in 1933, life in Göttingen changed completely when the Nazis came to power and Jewish lecturers were dismissed. By the autumn of 1933 most had left or were dismissed. Hilbert, although retired, had still

been giving a few lectures. In the winter semester of 1933–34 he gave one lecture a week on the foundations of geometry. After he finished giving this course, he never set foot in the institute again.

L. E. J. (Bertus) Brouwer (1881–1966)

Brouwer's most famous mathematical contribution was his "fixed-point theorem." As summarized in the introduction of the Wikipedia (2019a) article on the subject,

[a]mong hundreds of fixed-point theorems, Brouwer's is particularly well known, due in part to its use across numerous fields of mathematics. In its original field, the result is one of the key theorems characterizing the topology of Euclidean spaces. . . . This gives it a place among the fundamental theorems of topology. The theorem is also used for proving deep results about differential equations and is covered in most introductory courses on differential geometry. It appears in unlikely fields such as game theory. In economics, Brouwer's fixed-point theorem and its extension, the [Shizuo]Kakutani fixed-point theorem, play a central role in the proof of existence of general equilibrium in market economies as developed in the 1950s by economics Nobel Prize winners Kenneth Arrow and Gérard Debreu.

The general equilibrium models for which Brouwer's and Kakutani's fixed-point theorems "play a central role" include those of Von Neumann (1945–1946) and John Nash (1950). See also Scarf (1973).

As early as his doctoral dissertation, Brouwer showed an interest in mathematical analysis, of which his fixed-point theorem is the most important result, and views about the foundations of mathematics—which many found disturbing. He was advised to first build a reputation in mathematical analysis and then to publish his views on foundations. Wisely, that is what he did. By the time his foundational views became known, his credentials as a first-rate mathematician made it impossible to ignore his challenging ideas.

It is revealing to compare Brouwer and Hilbert, both in terms of how they were similar and how they differed. One similarity was their dedication to their craft. Neither had any physical or mental "disabilities" that would keep them from debating Hilbert's "formalism" versus Brouwer's" intuition-ism" on its merits or to refine their positions depending on the other's arguments.

We already noted that as of the turn of the nineteenth to twentieth century, Hilbert (1971, 1899) defined and illustrated what is now called "formalism." Brouwer's contribution, as quoted by MacTutor (2003a) from Geoffrey Kneebone, goes as follows:

Brouwer is most famous . . . for his contribution to the philosophy of mathematics and his attempt to

build up mathematics anew on an Intuitionist foun-
dation, in order to meet his own searching criticism
of hitherto unquestioned assumptions. Brouwer was
somewhat like Nietzsche in his ability to step outside
the established cultural tradition in order to subject
its most hallowed presuppositions to cool and objec-
tive scrutiny; and his questioning of principles of
thought led him to a Nietzschean revolution in the
domain of logic. He in fact rejected the universally
accepted logic of deductive reasoning which had been
codified initially by Aristotle, handed down with very
little change into modern times, and very recently
extended and generalized out of all recognition with
the aid of mathematical symbolism.

. . .

Brouwer's projected reconstruction of the whole
edifice of mathematics remained a dream, but his
ideal of constructivism is now woven into our whole
fabric of mathematical thought, and it has inspired,
as it still continues to inspire, a wide variety of inqui-
ries in the constructivist spirit which have let to major
advances in mathematical knowledge.

Hilbert was German, and Brouwer was Dutch. We already noted that when the Jews were expelled from Göttingen, Hilbert fulfilled one last obligation and never showed up again. Brower was part of the Dutch underground during the Nazi occupation and in that capacity helped Jews escape. When the Nazis required their version of a "loyalty oath," Brouwer encouraged his students to sign it so that they could learn math during the day and resist at night. Both Hilbert and Brouwer were greatly honored in their time. Even those on Hilbert's side of the argument understood the importance of Brouwer's challenge.

Brouwer was almost 20 years younger than Hilbert. Hilbert died during World War II. Brouwer died in 1966. MacTutor (2003a) relates his final years thus:

> *After retiring in 1951, Brouwer lectured in South Africa in 1952, and in the United States and Canada in 1953. His wife died in 1959 at the age of 89, and Brouwer, who himself was 78, was offered a one-year post in the University of British Columbia in Vancouver; he declined. In 1962, despite being well into his 80s, he was offered a post in Montana. He died in 1966 in Blaricum as the result of a traffic accident.*

Hilbert and his student John von Neumann epitomize rationality. Brouwer, however, was a mystic.

Hermann K. H. Weyl (1885–1955)

Weyl was a polymath. His MacTutor (2005b) biography includes many interesting details about his colorful life as part of the German intelligentsia in Germany before 1933. I will skip all this, except to note that his wife was Jewish; therefore, the Weyls moved from Göttingen to Princeton in 1933.

A few quotes from his MacTutor (2005b) biography will serve to characterize the opposition to Cantor's work.

Weyl certainly undertook work of major importance at Princeton, but his most productive period was without doubt the years he spent at Zurich. He attempted to incorporate electromagnetism into the geometric formalism of general relativity. He produced the first unified field theory for which the Maxwell electromagnetic field and the gravitational field appear as geometrical properties of space-time.

With his application of group theory to quantum mechanics he set up the modern subject.

. . .

Many other great books by Weyl appeared during his years at Princeton. These include Elementary Theory of Invariants *(1935),* The Classical Groups: Their Invariants and Representations *(1939),* Algebraic Theory of Numbers *(1940),* Philosophy of Mathematics and Natural Science *(1949),* Symmetry *(1952), and* The Concept of a Riemannian Surface *(1955). There is so much that could be said about all these works, but we restrict ourselves to looking at the contents of* Symmetry *for this perhaps tells us most about the full range of Weyl's interests.*

. . .

In Symmetry, *Weyl shows how the special theory of relativity is essentially the study of the inherent symmetry of the four-dimensional space-time continuum, where the symmetry operations are the Lorentz transformations; and how the symmetry operations of an atom, according to quantum mechanics, include the permutations of its peripheral electrons. Turning from physics to mathematics, he gives an extraordinarily concise epitome of Galois theory, leading up to the statement of his guiding principle: "Whenever you have to deal with a structure-endowed entity, try to determine its group of automorphisms."*

. . .

Weyl was much influenced by Edmund Husserl in his outlook and also shared many ideas with Brouwer. Both shared the view that the intuitive continuum is not accurately represented as a set-theoretic continuum.

Weyl's often-quoted comment is:

My work always tried to unite the truth with the beautiful, but when I had to choose one or the other, I usually chose the beautiful. . . .

Although half a joke, it sums up his personality.

CANTOR RECONSIDERED

I believe Cantor is correct. But when someone as brilliant and profound as Weyl rejects a belief of mine, it forces me to ask, why do I hold these beliefs? In particular, why do I believe Cantor?

Cantor's core insight from which modern mathematics unfolded, like a new human unfolding from a fertilized egg, was his "diagonal" argument that not all infinite sets can be placed in one-to-one correspondence with the natural numbers. This core insight consists of three concepts, namely,

1. An infinite sequence of zeros and ones,
2. The set of *all* infinite sequences of zeros and ones, and
3. Cantor's diagonal argument.

Let us examine each of these concepts in turn.

1. An Infinite Sequence of Zeros and Ones

Ignore here any interpretation of such a sequence as the binary expansion of a real number or the inclusions and exclusions of some subset of all integers. Think of it rather as perhaps a sequence of zeros and ones generated by repeated flips of a fair coin. Such infinitely repeated iids are the warp and woof of modern probability theory. How could I *not* think of such sequences as existing-in-principle.

2. The Set of All Such Sequences

Modern probability theory would view this as the "sample space" from which a point (i.e., a specific sequence) will be drawn. The whole space has a probability of one. The empty set has a probability of zero. The probability relationships among various subsets of this sample space will be reviewed in a later chapter.

How could I reject the concept of the set of *all* zero-one sequences?

3. Cantor's Diagonal Argument

Cantor asserts that the set of all such sequences is "uncountable." Look at sequence (14.8b). That's it! How can you *not* believe Cantor's diagonal argument and its conclusion?

Therefore, I stand with Cantor on this matter, as do Dedekind and Hilbert.

Henri Poincaré (1854–1912)

I have placed Poincaré's biography out of order to illustrate the dire consequence that can result from underrating Cantor's work. The noted and noteworthy Henri Poincaré, mathematician and physicist, was born at a critical time in the history of modern math, namely 9 years after Cantor was born and twelve years before Hilbert. Recall that Poincaré was one of the first mathematicians that Hilbert and Study visited in Paris. They must have gotten on well since Poincaré returned the visit a few days later. Recall also that the Poincaré book *Science and Hypothesis* (2012, 1902), cited in Chapter 13, was—and is—considered a great philosophical piece on scientific reasoning.

Poincaré considered Cantor's work a passing fad. Ironically, one of Poincaré's great mathematical creations was his work on "topology," the study of what properties of surfaces and solids remain unchanged under *continuous* transformations. Today, the standard text on topology is John Kelley's (1955) *General Topology*. According to Kelley,

> [t]his book is a systematic exposition of the part of general topology which has proven useful in several branches of mathematics. It is especially intended as background for modern analysis, and I have, with difficulty, been prevented by my friends from labeling it: What Every Young Analyst Should Know.

The most basic results in this area were assembled, systematized and extended by Felix Hausdorff (1957). In particular, Hausdorff's name is immortalized in the concept of a Hausdorff space, which Kelley covers, of course. Kelley does not mention Poincaré.

BROUWER'S OBJECTIONS

At the heart of the controversy of the Great Debate between Brouwer's "intuitionism" and Hilbert's "formalism" was whether Aristotle's law of the excluded middle—i.e., a proposition is either true or false—should be applied to infinite collections. In particular, according to Brouwer (1927), *[w]ithin a specific finite "main system" we can always test (that is, either prove or reduce to absurdity) properties of systems, that is, test whether systems can be mapped, with prescribed correspondences between elements, into other systems: for the mapping determined by the property in question can in any case be performed in only a finite number of ways, and each of these can be undertaken by itself and pursued either to its conclusion or to a point of inhibition.*

. . .

On the basis of the testability just mentioned, there had, for properties conceived within a specific finite main system, the principle of excluded middle, that is, the principle that for every system every property is either correct . . . or impossible, and in particular the principle of the reciprocity of the complementary species, that is, the principle that for every system the correctness of a property follows from the impossibility of the impossibility of this property.

. . .

An a priori *character was so consistently ascribed to the laws of theoretical logic that until recently these laws, including the principle of the excluded middle, were applied without reservation even in the mathematics of infinite systems, and we did not allow ourselves to be disturbed by the consideration that the results obtained in this way are in general not open, either practically or theoretically,*

to any empirical corroboration. On this basis, exten-
sive incorrect theories were constructed, especially in
the last half-century. . . . The following two funda-
mental properties, which follow from the principle of
the excluded middle, have been of basic significance
for this incorrect "logical" mathematics of infinity
("logical" because it makes use of the principle of the
excluded middle), especially for the theory of real
functions (developed mainly by the Paris school):

1. *The points of the continuum form an ordered point*
   species;

2. *Every mathematical species is either finite or*
   infinite.

According to Brouwer (1927),

[s]ets and elements of sets are called mathematical
entities.

By a species . . . of first order we understand a
property (defined in a conceptually complete form)
that only a mathematical entity can possess, and if it
does, the entity is called an element of the species of
first order. Sets constitute special cases of species of
first order.

Brouwer justifies his first claim that the real line is not an
"ordered species" as follows:

The following example shows that the first funda-
mental property is incorrect. Let d_v be the vth digit to
the right of the decimal point in the decimal expan-
sion of π, and let $m = k_n$ if, as the decimal expansion
of π is progressively written, it happens at d_m for the
nth time that the segment $d_m d_{m+1} \ldots d_{m+9}$ of this
decimal expansion forms the sequence 0123456789.
Further, let $c_v = (-1/2)^k{}_l$, otherwise let $c_n = (-1/2)^v$;
then the infinite sequence $c_1, c_2, c_3, \ldots$ defines a real
number r for which none of the conditions $r > 0$, $r =$
0, or $r < 0$ holds.

As to his second assertion that a species (i.e., a collection of some kind) is not necessarily finite or infinite, Brouwer
defends this thus:

That the second fundamental property is incorrect is
seen from the example provided by the species of the
positive integers kn defined above.

Brouwer's position generally may be stated more convention-
ally as, "The real numbers are not an ordered set."

I approach Brouwer's restrictions and their implications from two points of view. First, both formalism and intuitionism are in use today. Formalism rules the day as far as
advanced modern mathematics is concerned, including the
rigorous treatment of probability theory for nonfinite sample
spaces. But books and articles are written on results derivable

by the rules of intuitionism and other forms of "constructionism." See, in particular, Arend Heyting (1956) and Errett Bishop (1967). Thus, from the point of view of supporting differing logic systems, with differing axioms and permitted logical steps, I need to accommodate systems, including—but not confined to—those of Hilbert (1927), Brouwer (1927) as codified by Heyting (1959), and the constructionism of Bishop.

On the other hand, my own view of the matter is that any argument that concludes that the point on the line which is 3.1416 . . . d_n units from the origin (for some large n) does not exist until someone figures out its value is utter nonsense.

AXIOMATIC SET THEORY

Hilbert sought to axiomatize logic itself, as he had done for geometry in Hilbert (1971, 1899). This became known as "Hilbert's Program." It went through three phases:

- Before the Great Debate began,
- After the Great Debate began but before Kurt Gödel's two famous theorems, and
- After Gödel.

The events which separated Phase 1 from Phase 2 and Phase 2 from Phase 3 are recounted in later sections. Others also pursued an axiomatic approach to provide logic (i.e., the study of the "relationships among ideas") on a firm basis. We have already discussed Frege's "bug" and Russell's "fix." The remaining sections of this chapter will

- Briefly discuss the essence of the Peano Axioms (PAs);
- Discuss at length ZFC (Zermelo, Frankel, choice), the GAAS (Generally Accepted Axiom System) of logicians; and
- Discuss the limits of logic—i.e. the limits of "Pure Reason" presented in the works of Gödel and Thoralf Skolem.

PEANO'S AXIOMS (PAs)

Giuseppe Peano (1889), reproduced in *From Frege to Gödel* (1967), presented axioms for the "natural numbers," i.e., the nonnegative integers. These axioms are of two sorts: one kind are rules of logic; the others characterize the natural numbers (NNs). There is no need here to examine why ZFC became the GAAS of the field rather than those of Peano (see Exhibit 14.3). My own slight semantic restatement of Peano's Axioms refers to "a" natural number system rather than "the" natural numbers. I also speak of it as an SOS (Standard Ordered Set), as illustrated earlier in this chapter. If we let NNS stand for "natural number systems," then, in semi-SIMSCRIPT:

> Entity types include NNS and NNe
>
> Every NNS has a First NN.
>
> Every NN has a NEXT AND A PRIOR ATTRIBUTE
>
> If NN $\neq$ FIRST (NNS), Then Prior (NN) $\neq$ NULL

EXHIBIT 14.3 From Peano's Axioms

$$(1)\ S = Z^{+-} \qquad (X = 1.1)$$

the positive, zero and negative integers, and with

$$f(x, y) = f(y, x)$$
$$= x + y$$
$$= y + x \qquad \text{for all } x, y \in S = Z^{+-}$$

HILBERT'S PROGRAMS

The *Stanford Encyclopedia of Philosophy* article on "Hilbert's Program" notes that Hilbert's Program went through the previously noted three phases:

- First, Hilbert and colleagues tried to apply the same principles to logic as Hilbert applied to geometry in Hilbert (1971, 1899).
- The next was in response to Brouwer's objections.
- The third was in response to Gödel's results.

Brouwer held that a number does not exist unless someone has actually calculated it. Hilbert's approach *sounds* similar, but the difference is ever so important. Specifically,

> [t]he cornerstone of Hilbert's philosophy of mathematics, and the substantially new aspect of his foundational thought from 1922b onward, consisted in what he called the finitary standpoint. This methodological standpoint consists in restriction of mathematical

thought to those objects which are "intuitively present
as immediate experience prior to all thought," and to
those operations on and methods of reasoning about
such objects which do not require the introduction
of abstract concepts, in particular, without appeal to
completed infinite totalities. There are several basic
and interrelated issues in understanding Hilbert's
finitary standpoint:

1. *What are the objects of finitary reasoning?*
2. *What are the finitarily meaningful propositions?*
3. *What are the finitarily acceptable methods of*
   construction and reasoning?

My own views are in accord with Hilbert's views on deduction from axioms, as is the norm generally now. However, I note here that Hilbert's view of how axioms are to be selected "prior to all thought" is the opposite of the generally accepted Kantian view that the *a priori* is that which can be established by "Pure Reason" before any experience.

WHITEHEAD AND RUSSELL

The eminent Alfred Whitehead and the young Bertrand Russell carried out the tedious exercise of deriving arithmetic from logic. The method they espoused for avoiding Russell's paradox is Russell's "Theory of Types" (1908).

Specifically, on page 37 of Whitehead and Russell (1970, 1910) we are told that

> [a]n analysis of the paradoxes to be avoided shows that they all result from a certain kind of vicious circle. The vicious circles in question arise from supposing that a collection of objects may contain members which can only be defined by means of the collection as a whole. Thus, for example, the collection of propositions will be supposed to contain a proposition stating that "all propositions are either true or false." It would seem however, that such a statement could not be legitimate unless "all propositions" referred to some already definite collection, which it cannot do if new propositions are created by statements about "all propositions" are meaningless. More generally, given any set of objects such that, if we suppose the set to have a total, it will contain members which presuppose this total, then such a set cannot have a total. By saying that a set has "no total," we mean, primarily, that no significant statement can be made about "all its members." Propositions, as the above illustration shows, must be a set having no total. The same is true, as we shall shortly see, of propositional functions even when these are restricted to such as can significantly have as argument a given object a. In such cases, it is necessary to break up our set into

*smaller sets, each of which is capable of a total. This
is what the theory of types aims at effecting.*

*The principle which enables us to avoid illegiti-
mate totalities may be stated as follows: "Whatever
involves all of a collection must not be one of the collection"; or, conversely: "If, provided a certain collection
had a total, it would have numbers only definable in
terms of that total, then the said collection has no total."
We shall call this the "vicious-circle principle," because
it enables us to avoid the vicious circles involved in the
assumption of illegitimate totalities.*

Russell's "Theory of Types" proved to be unnecessarily
complicated. Simpler approaches soon followed. In particular, ZFC and an alternative proposed by von Neumann are the
currently "Generally Accept Axiom Systems." We will discuss
the former at length and the latter briefly.

ZERMELO'S AXIOMS

Exhibit 14.4 presents the seven axioms of Ernest Zermelo
(1908). Axioms I, II and IV provoked no objections. In particular, Axiom I tells any logic system of which it is a part that
a set is no more and no less than the collection of its members.
Axiom II tells the logic system about the null set and sets with
one and two specified members. Axiom IV tells the logic system of what Cantor calls the "power" set, namely the set of all
subsets of a given set.

EXHIBIT 14.4 Zermelo's Axioms

N	A set. Interpret as the Integers.
S	A larger set such that N ⊂ S interpret as the Real Numbers.
I	i ∈ N. Interpret "i" as an integer.
"∈," "="	Two operator symbols with their usual meanings
"+1"	An operator. Denoted below as S for "Successor."

Axioms

$$-m \neq n \text{ implies } S(m) \neq S(n)$$
$$-S(m) \neq S(n) \text{ implies } m \neq n$$

If $T \subset R$
   $1 \in T$
   $1 \in T \text{ implies } S(i) \, T$

Then $T = N$

The obvious problem with Axiom III is the vagueness of the requirement that a "propositional function" be "definite." How is one to know this? For example, if one writes a proof-checking computer program, how is one to check whether or not a propositional function is "definite"? This was spotted immediately by Zermelo's colleagues and fixed in the now-standard "ZFC." (Z is for "Zermelo;" F stands for "Fraenkel" and C is for "choice") axiom system.

Axioms I–V are true for finite- as well as infinite-dimensional spaces. Axiom VII rules out the possibility that the set of *all* sets is finite. Specifically, the axiom asserts that the null set, with no elements, is a set

$$\{\,\}$$

Further, there is also a set with one element, namely

$$\{\,\{\,\}\,\}$$

where the null set, itself, is considered an object that can belong to a set. The next step, in this ascending sequence of sets, is a set with two members, namely

$$\{\,\{\,\},\{\,\{\,\},\{\{\,\}\}\,\}\,\}\ \text{etc.}$$

THE "AXIOM OF CHOICE"

No one who understood what these axioms said—and was not dead set against axiom systems generally—raised any objections to Axioms I–V or VII. Axiom VI was another matter. A thoughtful examination by Zermelo of arguments by Cantor and others in deriving set-theoretical results revealed the implicit use of one rule of inference which Zermelo called the "Axiom of Choice." The legitimacy of its explicit use was disputed, even by those who had previously assumed it unknowingly.

Fraenkel's (1922) contribution—worthy of a letter in ZFC—was to show that the other six Zermelo axioms (with Axiom III fixed up, of course) are independent of Axiom VI. In other words, the six *other* axioms do not imply Axiom VI; nor does any four of them—plus Axiom VI—imply the left-out one of the other six. Furthermore, without Axiom VI, one *cannot* deduce Cantor's "theorem" that every set can be well-ordered. In fact, the well-ordering assumption and the axiom of choice are equivalent—each (plus the five other axioms) implies the other. A great many equivalents have been found over time, the most important of which, to my mind, is discussed in the next section.

But before we leave Zermelo's axioms as fixed up by Fraenkel, let us pause to admire their beauty and significance. Five of its axioms "explain" to a logic system what, in another context, would be considered definitions of the words "set," "subset," the "null set," etc. Adding Axiom VII captures all that Peano (1899) had to say about the *integers*. Adding Axiom VI implies Cantor's well-ordering "habit" and *everything* that the constructionist crowd is against.

THE TRICHOTOMY EQUIVALENT
TO THE AXIOM OF CHOICE

Axiom VI, the Axiom of Choice, has many "equivalents" in the sense that each of these "equivalents" is true *if and only if* Axiom VI, as well as Axioms I–V, is true. Thus, one can pick among the equivalents one finds most immediately intuitive as one's "Axiom VI." The one I find most compelling is the "Trichotomy" equivalent.

The sequence of sets, $\aleph_0$, $\aleph_1$, $\aleph_2$, ..., is clearly of increasing "size" in the sense that there is a subset of $\aleph_1$ that can be mapped one-to-one with the whole of $\aleph_0$, but no subset of $\aleph_0$ that can be mapped to the whole of $\aleph_1$; and the same is true for each successive aleph. You can see that; I can see that; but the ZF axioms without Axiom VI, the Axiom of Choice, cannot see that The Trichotomy equivalent says that given any two sets, S and T, either

$$S < T$$
$$S = T \quad \text{or}$$
$$S > T$$

in the sense that either a subset of T maps one-to-one into all S but not vice versa, or a subset of S maps one-to-one into all of T but not vice versa, or neither of the above. You see it, I can see it, but without Axiom VI, as well as Axioms I–V, the ZF axioms— without Axiom VI or an equivalent—do not know about it.

KURT GÖDEL (1906–1978)

Kurt had quite a happy childhood. He was very devoted to his mother but seemed rather timid and troubled when his mother was not in the home. He had rheumatic fever when he was six years old, but after he recovered life went on much as before. However, when he was eight years old he began to read medical books about the illness he had suffered from, and learnt that a weak heart was a possible complication. Although there is no evidence that he did have a weak heart, Kurt became convinced that he did, and concern for his health became an every-day worry for him. Kurt attended school in Brünn, completing his school studies in 1923. According to

> *MacTutor (2003b), his brother Rudolf said, "Even in High School my brother was somewhat more one-sided than me and to the astonishment of his teachers and fellow pupils had mastered university mathematics by his final Gymnasium years. . . . Mathematics and languages ranked well above literature and history. At the time it was rumored that in the whole of his time at High School not only was his work in Latin always given the top marks but that he had made not a single grammatical error."*

In the section on "Hilbert's Program," we noted that Hilbert twice redefined the objectives of his program: once under the influence of Brouwer's objection and then and again as the result of Gödel's results. Of Gödel's two papers on the subject, the second is most damning to Hilbert's original program. Early in Gödel (1931), the author describes in detail what he is about to prove.

THORALF SKOLEM (1887–1863)

In Skolem (1922), the author tells us that he will address the following eight issues:

1. The peculiar fact that, in order to treat of "sets," we must begin with "domains" that are constituted in a certain way;

2. A definition, much to be desired, that makes Zermelo's notion of "definite proposition" precise;

3. The fact that in every thoroughgoing axiomatization set-theoretic notions are unavoidably relative;

4. The fact that Zermelo's system of axioms is not sufficient to provide a foundation for ordinary set theory;

5. The difficulties caused by the nonpredicative stipulations when one wants to prove the consistency of the axioms;

6. The nonuniqueness (*Mehrdeutigkeit*) of the domain B;

7. The fact that mathematical induction is necessary for the logical investigation of abstractly given systems of axioms; and

8. A remark on the principle of choice.

Here I will only deal with Skolem's Items (3) and (4). To a large extent, the other six points are either preparation for or corollaries of Items (3) and (4). Of these two, Item (4) describes deficiencies of the Zermelo axioms specifically. Item 3 and its discussion demonstrates a remarkable limitation of *all* axiom systems. Therefore, I will discuss Item (4) first and then the world-altering Item (3) second.

According to Skolem, the ways in which "Zermelo's system is not sufficient . . . " are the following: Concerning Item (3), Skolem shows this: Suppose that one has an axiom system that satisfies Axiom VII, the Axiom of Infinite, which ensures that the number-set being described contains at least a countable number of members; and suppose further that one hopes to axiomatize Cantor's description of countable and uncountable sets and their associated cardinal and ordinal numbers. Skolem shows that if an axiom system can be satisfied by any infinite set of objects, it can be satisfied by a countable set. A system of axioms that can be satisfied *only* by its intended application is called "categorical." Skolem's Item (3) says that any attempt to characterize Cantor's hierarchy of infinities *cannot* be categorical.

Conclusion: Cantor's "diagonal argument" convinced most, including me, that there are noncountable sets, whereas Skolem shows that no set of axioms can characterize categorically the difference between countable and uncountable sets.

15

LOGIC IS PROGRAMMING IS LOGIC

INTRODUCTION

El Capitan is Yosemite National Park's most imposing structure. It rises about 3,000 feet "straight up." Its faces are white
and green. The white is granite, and the green is lichens starting the long, slow process of turning tall mountains into sand.
Typically, there are climbers on the face of the mountain, and
since (except for "power climbs") it is a many-day ascent,
some kind of stone nook is used on which to spend the nights
after suspending a mesh "cocoon" on two bolts driven into the
side of the mountain. The easier way is to drive to the top, get
out and look down.

I believe that leading mathematicians, starting with Frege
and Russell, climbed to the pinnacle of logical reasoning the
wrong way. Frege sought to derive *logic* from *set theory*. We
have seen the problems that leads to.

My approach, on the other hand, is simplicity itself.
Specifically, subsequent sections of this chapter present the

EAS (Entity, Attribute, Set) structure of number systems and the structures built out of them.

No contradiction can arise, since natural number systems exist, as must objects built "constructively" on them.

We begin with a brief comment on terminology.

TERMINOLOGY

Let us consider the sets of objects that appear in a SIMSCRIPT I, II, II.5 simulation or nonsimulation program. I leave SIMSCRIPT III off the list, since (as described in Chapter 12 in Volume II) for "marketing reasons" CACI has injected "object-oriented" programming into it, so SIMSCRIPT III is, as they say, "neither fish nor fowl nor good red herring."

When speaking or writing informally, I use the words "entities," "objects," and "things" interchangeably. For example, to my ear the word "objects" rolls off the tongue much more smoothly than does "entities." On the other hand, when describing formal systems, I will stick to the EAS terminology.

NUMBER SYSTEMS AND THE EAS STRUCTURES BUILT ON THEM

Thoreau famously said: "If a man does not keep pace with his companions, perhaps it is because he hears a different drummer. Let him step to the music which he hears, however measured or far away." In particular, my definition of a *natural number* differs radically from those of the mathematical giants whose accomplishments arc infinitely beyond those to which I could aspire. Nevertheless, I consider my definition to be as valid as theirs and clearly superior in its ease of understanding. As should be no surprise by now, my construction consists of EAS structures based on Standard Ordered Sets. (SOSs). I see two general types of basic kinds of things in the present situation, namely

A. SOSs and their contents, such as the marks on a bone or the Indo-Arabic number system, and

B. Propositions, i.e., statements which are either true or false.

If a statement can be other than true or false—e.g., if it needs to have certain terms specified before it is a "proposition" as Aristotle used the term, and as I will here—then it is *not* a proposition. Rather, it is a *proposition function,* which becomes a proposition when its arguments (inputs) are specified.

In our specific case, the propositions referred to in Item (B) include propositions about SOSs and their members. It also includes propositions about systems of propositions. An example of the former is the PAs (Peano Axioms) for the integers, whereas the most famous propositions about propositions are those of Gödel. See Chapter 14 concerning the Peano Axioms and Gödel's theorems.

Russell (1908) defines a number to be the set of all sets that can be placed in one-to-one correspondence to each other. The notion that a number should be defined in terms of "set-concepts" rather than the properties shared, e.g., by (1) marks on bones and (2) the Indo-Arabic number system, is held generally by mathematicians concerned with foundations. As I said in the Introduction to this chapter, this seems to me to be the hard way to ascend this El Capitan.

The way I see it, any SOS is an "Integer *System*." An *integer* is any member of the set of all integers owned by *The System*. I would no more speak of *the* integers than I would speak of *the* job shops. For me, integers belong to integer systems just as jobs belong to job shop systems.

In the section that follows I will describe integer systems, systems built on integer systems, propositions, and systems of propositions about systems of propositions built on integer systems, in terms of the entities, attributes, and sets involved. Generally, I find that the EAS-E worldview is

> *A view with which,*
> *To model many things:*
> *Shoes and Ships and Sealing Wax,*
> *And Cabbages and Kings;*
> *And what makes JobShops run the best;*
> *And whether thoughts have wings.*

DEDUCTIVE SYSTEMS AS PROGRAMMING LANGUAGES

The rules of a deductive system are, in effect, the rules of programming languages. Specifically, they instruct a human or computer as to how it is permitted to change the state of some kind of human, machine, or printed page's "memory." For concreteness, suppose that the "memory" is stored in a modern computer database. Its contents are *propositions* and their *proofs,* where required. Initially, the database contains unproven propositions taken as *axioms* involving not-otherwise-defined terms. From time to time new propositions are added to the database, either as *definitions* of new terms or as *theorems,* which follow from existing propositions by *permitted steps.* The kinds of steps that are permitted may be specified as part of the axioms of the particular deductive system. For example, Logical Expression (14.1) in Chapter 14 could be written in a form more convenient for computer processing, such as

$$(A \rightarrow B \ \& \ A) \Rightarrow B \qquad (15.1)$$

and taken as an axiom of logic.

In Logical Expression (15.1) the symbol "$\rightarrow$"represents what is called a "material implication" such as "being human" implies "being mortal," whereas the "$\Rightarrow$" symbol represents the logical implication, i.e., the proposition that follows "$\Rightarrow$" follows logically from one or more statements that precede "$\Rightarrow$."

At this point it is easy to see the difference between "Logic" and "Metalogic." Proposition (15.1) is typically an axiom in a "Logic Database," whereas the "programming procedure" ("permitted steps") that it describes is a procedure that must be added to a standard SIMSCRIPT or EAS-E System to make it a "deductive system."

A VARIETY OF DEDUCTIVE DSSs

Historically, the "memory" used to record the axioms and their consequences of some branch of mathematics has been the printed page. For example, Hilbert's history-making volume, *The Foundations of Geometry*, is a prototypical. The Whitehead and Russell (1970) three-printed-volume axiomatic derivation of the laws of logic and arithmetic is another.

One of the original applications of AI (Artificial Intelligence) was Newell, Shaw and Simon's (NSS; 1957) computerized version of Volume I of the aforementioned Whitehead and Russell (1970). NSS's other work (e.g., NSS; 1958) used the computer to play chess. As computers became more powerful, the computing profession, e.g., IBM Corporation with its Big Blue, used this ever-growing memory and computing power to match the best of the computers against the best of human chess players. On the other hand, little if anything has been done to pursue the other NSS goal, namely the use of computers to prove theorems.

Importantly, NSS did *not* use AI to prove theorems that had not been proved before. Rather, they used their procedures to prove some of the same theorems that Whitehead and Russell had proved. Their objective was "proof of concept": to show that their formalized AI procedures could perform tasks that only humans had done before. A team comparable to the

Big Blue team—that "coached" the IBM supercomputer on how to play chess—could undertake the task of comparable scope to "coach" a more recent supercomputer to find further implications of the Whitehead and Russell (WR) axioms using the WR rules of deduction. Such an undertaking would present enormous challenges and opportunities. The ultimate goal of such an undertaking would be to find important new theorems in some area-of-interest. To a certain extent, it would operate "on its own," as programmed, of course, seeking theorems that humans-in-the-field would consider important. But it should be open to suggestions from the finest minds in the field or from curious amateurs. It could check out any number of suggestions, perhaps combining different suggestions in its approach to solving great unsolved problems.

A logic DSS would include theorems and their proofs, and for each step in a proof, the DSS must either remember or be able to confirm the reason the step is permitted. As already noted, access to such information could be useful to both novice and expert. The query capabilities of the DSS should permit the *novice* to get a spelled-out version of some proof that his or her introductory text presents too compactly or with insufficient rigor. The DSS should also permit the expert to better understand why one proposition is derivable from one set of axioms, using one set of inference rules, whereas the same proposition cannot be derived from a slightly different set of axioms or a slightly different set of inference rules.

One challenge is how does one build such a logic DSS? This will be the principal topic for the remainder of this chapter.

ALTERNATIVE RULES OF INFERENCE

Rules of inference are sometimes viewed as "axioms about axiom systems" and presented symbolically, such as the following: Let "$\Rightarrow$" stand for "A implies B" or, equivalently, "If A then B." Also, let "&" stand for "and." Then the *modus ponens* axiom would be written as in Statement (15.1).

In words:

If A, then B
And A is true
Then we may conclude that
B is true.

The issue is not whether or not B is true, but whether it can be deduced from axioms and already-proved theorems stored in some form of memory.

As already noted, traditionally "memory" consisted of ink on paper, first handwritten and then set in type and printed in journals and books. One scholar would read the theorems and proofs of others, conceive new theorems, and, in turn, write them up for publication. It has long become impractical to write out complete, step-by-step proofs as Euclid did. This created three major problems:

1. It is sometimes found that incomplete proofs have bugs in them.

2. I imagine that I am not the only one who has tried to follow a printed mathematical derivation and

cannot figure out—for the life of me—how the author expects me to get to Statement (N) from its predecessor statements.

3. The compact notation of so-called "symbolic logic" is often very useful, but the view that this notation is essential for rigorous deduction is *wrong and harmful.*

 Its wrongfulness is evidenced by the rigorous writings of the ancient Greeks, including Aristotle, Euclid and Archimedes. Hilbert's complaint about Euclid was *not* that successive steps in his proofs did not have sufficient logical justification but that he failed to distinguish between an informal description of the *role* of words such as "point" and "line" in its *intended application,* as opposed to the way he tried to *define* all terms, including "point" and "line," in his formal axiom system. As Hilbert explains and illustrates, every axiom system must have undefined terms.

The harmfulness of the view that rigor requires arcane symbols is that it precludes the possibility of a database of theorems and proofs all in plain English. With modern computer technology one can have it both ways, symbolically or verbally, with the system-user having the ability to go back and forth between these two as the user needs or desires.

"LADDERS" AND "FIRE ESCAPES"

A "physical-world" ladder consists of a sequence (a.k.a. "ordered set") of rungs. Specifically, there is a first rung followed by a second higher rung, etc. up to the topmost rung of the ladder. The integers form a ladder with a first rung, a second, and so on; but they have no top rung. They ascend without end.

In the physical world as well as in the "conceptual world," one may consider the ladder as a whole as compared to a particular rung or set of rungs of the ladder—i.e., one can distinguish between "the ladder" and "all its rungs."

Moderately tall buildings in cities have "fire escapes." A fire escape always has a ladder that goes from the second floor to the ground floor. It is weighted so that it is horizontal until one goes to walk *down* it. Then it rotates to a descending staircase angle. There is another weighted ladder that goes from the third floor to the second; still another that goes from the fourth floor, if there is one, to the third. As before, physical fire escapes extend upward for a finite number of floors. Conceptual fire escapes need not.

But what EAS structure is shared by all such ladders and fire escapes? Speaking "informal" SIMSCRIPT, every ladder owns a set of rungs. If the ladder has any rungs at all (circus clown ladders might have none), the ladder has a first rung, and each rung in the ladder has a next-in-ladder attribute. If a rung has no next-in-ladder, then the next-in-ladder attribute is "null." By the Axiom of Choice, any set can be well-ordered. In particular, it can be a well-ordered set of ladders—which we have called a fire escape—and can contain well-ordered sets of any kind. All these encompass the kinds of things that Cantor envisioned. All are "constructed" with objects that trace their parentage to some integer system.

ORGANON 2000: FROM ANCIENT GREEK TO "SYMBOLIC LOGIC"

Since Aristotle mostly lectured rather than writing down his ideas in full, what we have are mostly his students' lecture notes, arranged into "books." Other Aristotle admirers arranged Aristotle's "books" into what seemed to be a logical order from a publisher's point of view. Stephen Cole Kleene (1971) says that

> Hilbert . . . draws a distinction between "real" and "ideal" statements in classical mathematics, in essence as follows. The real statements are those which are being used as having an intuitive meaning; the ideal statements are those which are not being so used. The statements which correspond to the treatment of the infinite as actual are ideal. Classical mathematics adjoins the ideal statements to the real, in order to retain the simple rules of the Aristotelian logic in reasoning about infinite sets.

On the other hand,

For every man, m: P(m) is true

is the same as

if m is a man, *then* P(m) is true

Thus, once the "is a" relationship is recognized, "quantification" adds nothing new.

SO, WHAT'S NEW?

Aristotle lectured. His students took notes. Someone, perhaps Aristotle himself in part, organized the lectures into books, and then the same or other people organized the books into series. In particular, the six books that comprise the Organon are

1. *Categories*
2. *On Interpretation*
3. *Prior Analytics*
4. *Posterior Analytics*
5. *Topics*
6. *Sophistical Refutations*

The third famously explores the syllogism. The modern treatment is more compact and computerized. This makes it more useful but not different.

The first two books of Aristotle's Organon examine the objects that can appear in a syllogism. Here Aristotle and I differ. Aristotle speaks of the role of the *words* that can appear in a syllogism. I speak of propositions concerning the attribute values of the entities including, perhaps, attribute's set membership. This distinction is subtle but important. For example, Alfred Tarski (1995) says that there are two basic principles of logic, namely "modus ponens" and "substitution." In the spirit of Whitehead and Russell, or even Hilbert before them, the "substitution rule" in Tarski's system describes a permitted step in a formal system without regard to the "meaning" of the form. My justification for so-called substitution is different. Consider the prototypical syllogism

All men are mortal
Socrates is a man
therefore
Socrates is mortal

In EAS-E terms, one attribute an individual can have is its "immortality"; said differently, the value of the Boolean attribute Is Immortal (i) is either TRUE (is immortal) or FALSE (is *not* immortal, i.e., is mortal). As Aristotle's "law of the excluded middle," *where applicable*, the variable the entity referenced by the letter "i" is of a type such that, if it exists of course, is either alive or dead.

The preceding entails some substitutability among propositions P and ¬P, since the excluded middle principle may be stated as

$$P = \neg\,(\neg P)$$

The substitution principle to which Tarski refers goes like the following:

$$\text{Socrates} = \text{Plato's Spokesperson}$$

Now consider any propositional function, i.e., a function whose input argument is an object of some specified type or types and whose output value is either TRUE or FALSE. In this instance, the inputs could be a great variety of types including Rocks, Robots, Rabbits, and Philosophers. Specifically,

$$\text{Is Immortal (Socrates)}$$

was FALSE as soon as he was conceived and remains true today if IsA includes WasA, WillB, Would have been, etc.

Now, because of the fact recounted by Equation (15.1), all the above is also true of "Plato's Spokesperson, i.e.,

$$\text{P (Socrates)} = \text{P (Plato's Spokesperson)}$$

where P stands for the propositional function in question to which Socrates can be an argument, because "Socrates" and "Plato's Spokesperson" are one and the same person and, as Shakespeare's Juliet might have put it, "Socrates by any other name is just as mortal."

IMMEDIATE CONSEQUENCES

IF *i* is a man, THEN *i* is mortal
Socrates is a man
Therefore, Socrates is mortal

Thus, the syllogism itself is a tautology, an example of a specific instance of a general rule.

TWO TYPES OF SET OWNERSHIP

The proposed SIMSCRIPT M, described in Chapter 12 (Volume II), distinguishes between sets whose members are *contained* in the set and those whose members are "physically" elsewhere. I speak here of the world represented by an EAS description. How this is stored in a computer memory is of no concern in this context.

While the rules for SIMSCRIPT M have not been written, a sensible set of rules would specify that a list of references can reference itself, whereas a set of (e.g.) boxes of various sizes, one inside the other, cannot have a box that is physically inside itself.

In the physical world there is always a largest such box. In the conceptual world, if there is a set of *all* such boxes, that too is a box. It may be given a different name. For example, if one had a system of boxes of size 1, 2, 3, . . . , then the containing box would be of $\aleph$. In any case, the idea that a physical entity contains itself directly or indirectly, such as A contains B contains C contains A, is *absurd* and must be considered a programming bug.

In short, Russell's paradox is a valid criticism of Frege's logic, but nothing "sophisticated" is needed to not fall into that trap.

MODELING MODELING

There are distinctions which no one would fail to make when modeling a job shop or a fighter-bomber war game but that one might fail to make when modeling the modeling process itself. Specifically, it is essential to carefully distinguish between the entities being modeled and the model of them. In particular, many great minds who sought to "modernize" Aristotle failed to make these distinctions, resulting in the equivalent of a Keystone Cops confusion. Let us examine these distinctions with care.

(1) The Model versus the Modeler versus the Modeled.

When I modeled the Market Simulator described in Chapter 7 (in Volume II), I always knew the difference between who was the modeler (me), the object being modeled (the stock market), and the model itself (JLMSim). "The model" has an EAS-E status and event description. It is not any specific securities market but a stylized version of "Securities Markets" in general. Thus "Securities Markets" are its IGA (Intended General Application). And thus, I was the Modeler, "stock markets" were the object modeled, and JLMS I.0 was the model.

(2) The Same Distinctions Must Be Kept in Mind When Modeler A Models Modeler B Modeling Entity Type C.

For example, suppose I build a logic system equivalent to Frege's, but substituting ASCII equivalents for Frege's logical-flow diagram notation, and derive Russell's Paradox from the Frege-equivalent axioms, then clearly I am the modeler, the Frege-system is the object modeled, and the model itself would be a Rady-EAS-E program.

EAS-E DEDUCTION: STATUS

Time changes some things and not others. For example, "Aristotelian logic" will remain "Aristotelian logic" forever. On the other hand, the possibility of adding specialized features to an existing general-purpose programming language to produce a "logic language" to facilitate a "logic" database has evolved. Specifically, Alasdar Mullarney, formerly the head of the CACI Research Department, now retired from CACI. I call it the "Rady-EAS-E" as opposed to the IBM-EAS-E since further work by graduate students at the Rady School at UCSD will be financed by a three-million-dollar fund of which one million was contributed by Ernest and Evelyn Rady.

To the Radys, as well to Tony Batman, sponsor of this book, as well as to my clients and other friends and well-wishers, I can say, "Thanks. I'll do my best."

16

THE INFINITE AND
THE INFINITESIMAL

POINTS AND LINES

Euclid characterized a line as having length but "no width" and a point as having "neither length nor width." He finessed the question of how one combines things with *no* width to form something *with* width. Zeno's paradox explores the mysteries of infinite divisibility. Archimedes computed areas and volumes by the method of exhaustion, e.g., by approximating the area of a circle by those of polygons whose areas approach that of the circle.

Man's understanding of the infinitesimal changed little from Archimedes' time until that of Newton and Leibnitz. The approaches of the latter two mental giants were quite different, as reflected in their notation. As described in Chapter 14, Newton thought and spoke of an instantaneous rate of speed, $X(t)$. He described this informally as a limit process. This was subsequently defined formally by the Weierstrass definition of a limit.

In contrast, Leibnitz wrote of infinitesimals as in the relationship

$$df = \frac{df}{dx}\,dx \qquad (16.1)$$

where df/dx is now interpreted as a limit of finite differences

$$\Delta f/\Delta X$$

Abraham Robinson (1974) showed that one can build a rigorous logical system in support of the concept of infinitesimals. Specifically, he built upon the "transfer principle" developed by Jerzy Łoś (pronounced "wash") that made infinitesimal analysis a powerful, practical tool. In particular, the transfer principle allows us to easily generalize to *infinite-dimensional* spaces the results on expected utility and personal probability developed in Markowitz (1959) for *finite*-dimensional spaces. However, the transfer principle uses the concept of an "internal set," which is quite subtle.

When I went to illustrate the points involved, it struck me that there was a much simpler path up this particular mountain. This was the result of combining two familiar concepts, namely

1. Cantor's extension of the (finite) "natural numbers" to the transfinite ordinal numbers, and
2. The process by which one goes from the natural numbers, to the integers, to the rational numbers, and finally to the reals.

Process (1) was described in Chapter 15. Process (2) involves the concept of a "complete field." This is discussed in the next section. This chapter itself is by far the shortest in the book. I have left it as a separate chapter rather than combining it with an adjacent larger chapter because this particular "mountain" demands a chapter of its own, whether or not it sports a four-lane highway to its top above the clouds.

FIELDS

The word "field" has multiple uses in mathematics, including

A. The field of mathematics that one works in;
B. The field equations, such as those by which electromagnetic waves propagate; and
C. The algebraic structure called a field.

The definition of the latter will be discussed shortly. One can check that the real numbers are a field, since they have all the properties that define an algebraic structure to be such. But the rational numbers also satisfy all the propositions that define a field. On the other hand, as we have already discussed, the rational numbers are not a *complete* field since, e.g., they do not contain any member whose square is 2. We can complete the field by Dedekind cuts, as explained in Chapter 14.

The preceding process starts with an SOS (Standard Ordered Set), i.e., a set with a first member and, for each member of the set, a next member. As Cantor demonstrated, such sets are not all "the same size," in the sense of the mathematical existence of a one-to-one correspondence between them. In particular, the "power set," namely, the set of all subsets of a given set, S, cannot be so related, as the "diagonal analysis" shows. But, as Gödel and Skolem showed, not every mathematical relationship that is surely true can be proved formally.

In short, inevitably and inescapably, words fail us.

CONSTRUCTING THE INFINITESIMALS

Let us repeat Process (2) mentioned earlier, by which one moves from the integers to the reals, but now apply it to the transfinite ordinals.

- **Step 1.** The first step in going from the integers to the reals is to consider what one obtains if one "imbeds" the integers into the "smallest field" which can include them. Since a field contains an inverse a^{-1} for each nonzero member a, a field containing the integers 1, 2, 3, . . . must also contain their inverses 1, $\frac{1}{2}$, $\frac{1}{3}$, . . . , as well as algebraic operations involving them.
- **Step 2.** If "u" is any transfinite number, therefore larger than any finite c, i.e.,

$$u > c > 0 \qquad (16.2a)$$

then its inverse must be smaller than any finite real number.

$$c^{-1} > u^{-1} > 0 \qquad\qquad (16.2b)$$

We can designate one of the infinitesimal quantities, $\epsilon > 0$, to be the inverse of some arbitrarily chosen infinite u.

One might see the following as a problem: the number system generated by the preceding process has finite numbers and transfinite numbers—but never the twain shall meet. *What connects the two number realms?* No problem: It is just a transfinite Dedekind cut. Dedekind settled the Pythagorean problem that there was no rational number whose squares equaled 2, by "constructing" the real numbers as "cuts" between two sets of rationals. We can similarly define the transfinite reals to be Dedekind cuts among the transfinite rationals. In particular, the "cut" that separates the finite rationals and the infinite ones is indeed a Dedekind cut, with one subset of this ordered set all below and all the others above the cut. Arithmetic continues to be defined to be a cut which separates the sum, product or inverse of the cut or cuts involved, and the same formal proof demonstrates the constancy of these definitions assuming that arithmetic itself is consistent.

This process produces all the infinite and infinitesimal magnitudes we may need without the pain of Nonstandard Analysis.

INFINITE-DIMENSIONAL UTILITY ANALYSIS

Chapters 10, 11, and 12 of Markowitz (1959) derived the EU (Expected Utility) and the EUPB (Expected Utility Probability Beliefs) rules, which assume that there was a *finite* M and N number of *outcomes* to the decision situation and possible "hypotheses" about *the world*. These are severe limitations on the generality of the analysis. Frequently one assumes that the outcome of a financial bet is a "return," where the latter is a *continuous* random variable, and the one or more hypotheses about the world that the analysis admits include at least one *continuous* parameter. One of the attractions of Nonstandard Analysis was its ability to generalize from finite to infinite N.

On second thought, I see that Cantor's transfinite induction was already a sufficient tool to demonstrate that what is true for the finite goose is also true for the transfinite gander.

THE ALGEBRAIC STRUCTURE CALLED "A FIELD"

A "field" is a set of points, F, endowed with two binary operators "+" and "·". The latter is commonly represented by juxtaposition, i.e.,

$$a \cdot b = ab$$

The two operators are *commutative, associative* and *distributive*, i.e.,

$$ab = ba$$

$$a + b = b + a$$
$$(ab) c = a (bc)$$
$$(a + b) + c = a + (b + c)$$
$$a (b + c) = ab + ac$$

It has additive and multiplicative identities:

$$1a = a$$
$$0 + a = a$$

Every number has an additive inverse, and every number except zero has a multiplicative inverse, i.e., for every a there is a b such that

$$a + b = 0$$

And for every a except 0 there is a b such that

$$ab = 1$$

The rational, real and complex numbers are fields. There are also finite fields involving the "modulus" operator

$$a \bmod b$$

The latter are presented in texts on abstract algebra and will not be discussed here.

17

INDUCTION THEORY

INTRODUCTION

In his classic book entitled *Risk, Uncertainty and Profit*, Frank H. Knight (1921) distinguishes between two kinds of situations commonly referred to as "risky," namely

- Ones in which odds are *measurable*, such as the outcome of a bet on a roll of fair dice;
- Ones in which there are no measurable odds, such as the outcome of a bet on a start-up company offering a new product.

Specifically, Knight (page 19) tells us:

The essential fact is that "risk" means in some cases a quantity susceptible of measurement, while at other times it is something distinctly not of this character; and there are far-reaching and crucial differences in the bearings of the phenomenon depending on which of the two is really present and operating. . . . It will appear that a measurable *uncertainty, or "risk" proper, as we shall use the term, is so far different from an* unmeasurable *one that is not in effect an uncertainty at all. We shall accordingly restrict the term "uncertainty" to cases of the nonquantitative type.*

I characterize the present volume as dealing with situations in which there are "no *known* odds," as distinguished from situations in which the odds are known, as analyzed in Volumes I and II. For brevity, I will refer to Volumes I and II as analyzing *risk* situations and the current volume as analyzing *uncertainty* situations. Note, however, that my use of the word "uncertainty" is broader than that of Knight. For me, "uncertain" is shorthand for "The decision maker does not *know* the odds for all relevant events." This includes cases in which there are no odds to know, such as the bet on a start-up company, and those in which there are odds in fact but they are not known, such as with a bet on a coin of questionable fairness.

The present chapter compares the following three models of rational decision-making under uncertainty (as I use the term, of course):

1. One is essentially the model presented in Markowitz (1959), Chapter 12. The weasel-word "essentially" refers to Endnote 1, cited in connection with Axiom I. Specifically, Axiom I here has three parts—(Ia), (Ib) and (Ic)—whereas that in Markowitz (1959) includes

a fourth part, (Id). The latter part is nonessential. It was there so that I could carry through a proof. Now I provide a different proof that does not require this excess baggage.

2. Model (1) was itself based on Savage (1954). To avoid confusion, I will denote the model in Markowitz (1959) as M59, as opposed to S54, presented in Savage (1954).

3. M59 is defined by four axioms, i.e., Axioms I–IV. The third RDM model presented here is M59 sans Axiom III. I label it M59X.

Later I will examine the differences between S54, M59 and M59X, and trace the thought-processes that lead from S54 to M59 to M59X. But first we should review where we are and how we got here in our philosophical journey.

THE STORY THUS FAR

Chapter 13 examined the views of various philosophers on three basic questions, namely

- What kinds of things can we know?
- How do we obtain this knowledge?
- How should this knowledge affect our action?

The focal point of that chapter was Hume's distinction between

- Logical relationships,
- Empirical relationships, and
- Value judgments.

In retrospect, we see that Aristotle got there first, and more thoroughly than Hume. Specifically, Aristotle's *Prior Analytics* defined what is now called "Aristotelean logic"; his *Posterior Analytics* anticipated the intuition that Bayesian analysis formalizes; and Aristotle's *Nicomachean Ethics* is still one of the major ethical pieces of western civilization.

Hilbert wanted to use logic to model logic, as he had used logic to model the objects and relationships of geometry. In particular, he wanted to *prove* that logic was complete and consistent and that any proposition implied by such a consistent set of axioms could be formally deduced within that system. But Gödel showed that this is impossible.

Charles Peirce's (1955) formulation of the induction problem added "randomness" and "probability relationships" to the mix. Specifically, Peirce says that the "kernel of pragmatism" is

> *that certain kinds of events would happen, one in so often, in the course of experience, under certain kinds of existential conditions—provided it can be proved to be true.*

Peirce stood on the shoulders of Alexander Bain (2004). Whether or not it is a universal principle applicable without exception, as far as the applications in this volume are concerned, I accept Bain's dictum:

> Is, or is not, Belief essentially related to Action, that is, Volition? Answer: It is. Preparedness to act upon what we affirm is admitted on all hands to be the sole, the genuine, and the unmistakable criterion of belief.

As to how to decide whether a given probabilistic statement can be proved, twentieth-century thought went through two revolutions—or, perhaps more precisely, a revolution and a counter-revolution. The revolution was R. A. Fisher's (1960) rejection of the use of Bayes's rule for what Fisher called "Inverse Probability." The counterrevolution was L. J. Savage's (1954) reinstatement of Bayes's rule, based on an axiomatic approach to rational decision-making.

The Savage axioms concern the actions of a Rational Decision-Maker (RDM). The implication of these axioms is that an RDM, acting according to them, would act as if it assigned "utility" numbers to what I call "outcomes" (Savage called them "consequences"), or "subjective probabilities" to what I call "hypotheses" (he called them "states"), and would act according to the EU/PB (expected utility/personal probability) maxim. Since Savage's "subjective" probabilities obey the same rules as do "objective" probabilities, the rules for conditional probabilities explored at length in Chapter 8 apply here equally. In this context, Equation (8.8) in Chapter

8 (in Volume II) is referred to as "Bayes's rule." The formula in Equation (8.12) is that for the "conditional probability" for one set of possible outcomes of a random event given that the actual outcome is known to be a member of another such set. One is not called a Bayesian because one believes in and applies this probabilistic truth. Rather, it is because one believes that one should act according to "subjective probabilities" that follow the same "laws of probability" that apply to "objective" probabilities, including Bayes's rule in particular.

Savage's arguments in favor of subjective probability were sufficiently compelling that a great many statisticians are now convinced that insofar as Fisher and his followers' "objective" statistical procedures conflict with those of Gauss (maximum likelihood), de Finetti's (1968) "personal probability beliefs" and Savage's (1954) axiomatic justification of the latter—it is Fisher's so-called objective procedures that are in error.

In terms of the Aristotle/Hume trichotomy concerning three types of assertions—matters of fact, relationships between ideas, and value judgments—the S54, M59 and M59X axioms and their consequences are, in themselves, relationships between ideas. A hypothesis that Human Decision-Makers (HDMs) act in accordance with one or another of these axiom systems, or that markets worked *as if* HDMs acted that way, is an assertion about matters of fact. Since RDMs are fictional beings, like Harry Potter and Superman, the assertion that an RDM acts this way defines *that* sort of RDM and is thus part of the relationships among ideas. The assertion that Human Decision-Makers (HDMs) *should* act this way is a value judgment.

CONCEPTS

This section and the next introduce and illustrate concepts and notation used in M59 and, consequently, in M59X. In particular, this section defines the words (and phrases) "outcome," "decision," "preferences between decisions," and "hypotheses about the nature of the world" as these terms are used in M59. Since M59 and M59X are identical except for the omission of M59's Axiom III, I will refer to these two concepts simply as those of M59.

As Hilbert explained, one must distinguish between a formal model and applications of such a model. The formal M59 model postulates an order relationship among certain m × n matrices. It also gives names to the entity-types represented by the rows, columns, and entries of these matrices and the matrices themselves. These names reflect the IGA (Intended General Application) of the model.

In Exhibit 17.1, the entities represented by the *rows* of the M59 matrices are what we will call "outcomes." They can be described (not *defined*, but described) as "that for which an RDM seeks a good probability distribution." More specifically, M59 is applicable to *many-period* financial decision situations of which the *single-period* situation is a special case.

EXHIBIT 17.1 Illustrative Decision Tables

	1	2	3	4	5	6	7
1	1	1	1	0	0	0	0
2	0	0	0	1	1	1	1

(17.1a)

	1	2	3	4	5	6	7
1	0	0	0	1	1	1	1
2	1	1	1	0	0	0	0

(17.1b)

	1	2	3	4	5	6	7
1	½	½	½	½	½	½	½
2	½	½	½	½	½	½	½

(17.1c)

For the present application—as that in Chapter 8 (in Volume II)—an "outcome" is a "consumption" time-sequence, *perhaps* represented as a series of money expenditures, perhaps deflated. Also, as in Chapter 8, the M59 choice-model assumes that there are a finite number of possible outcomes, one and only one of which will occur. But as we just saw in Chapter 16, logical relationships that hold among the finite integers and the complete field of real numbers generated by them also hold for the transfinite "integers" and their associated transfinite reals.

The columns of the $m \times n$ matrices represent hypotheses about how the world works, one and only one of which is true.

The $m \times n$ matrices, themselves, of M59 will be referred to as "decision matrices" or just "decisions." As in Chapter 8, a "decision" is the choice of a complete strategy that starts "now" and continues until "the end." It may also include randomization, e.g., as in a two-person game or agricultural experiments.

I will refer to the p_{ij}^d entry of a decision matrix, d, as the "objective" probability that outcome i will occur if hypothesis j is true. In Frank H. Knight's terminology, if a particular hypothesis was known to be true, the occurrence of possible outcomes would constitute a "risk" situation. In the terminology of the M59 IGA, choice when the true hypothesis is *not known* is an "uncertainty" situation. A prototypical application of M59 would be one in which the columns represent alternative hypotheses concerning the joint distribution of security or asset class returns, the rows represent different levels of expected return on the portfolio-as-a-whole, and the decision matrix is a consequence of the portfolio chosen.

There are, however, quite reasonable applications of M59 in which the P_{ij}^d entries are themselves subjective. If the analysis is applied to a question such as whether a particular financial advisor is honest or a crook, one column of the $d = (p_{ij}^d)$ matrix would represent the "honest" hypothesis and another the "crook" hypothesis. The p_{ij}^d entries associated with decision (d) would reflect one's intuitive estimates of the probability of certain observed behavior if the advisor is honest or a crook. In such a situation, the so-called objective probabilities, p_{ij}^d, are themselves subjective.

BASIC RELATIONSHIPS

In Chapters 1 (Volume I) and 8 (Volume II) we interpreted

$$P^3 = pP^1 + (1 - p)\, P^2 \qquad (17.1a)$$

as the probability distribution which results if one randomly chooses—with probability p versus (1 − p)—between the strategy that yields probability distribution P^1 versus one that yields P^2. M59 similarly interprets the matrix

$$d^3 = pd^1 + (1 - p)\, d^2 \qquad (17.1b)$$

to be the d-matrix that results if one randomly chooses between the strategy that yields d^1 and that which yields d^2. The reasoning here is that if hypothesis j is true, then—letting P_j^1 and P_j^2 be the jth columns of d^1 and d^2, respectively—

$$P_j^3 = pP_j^1 + (1 - p)P_j^2 \qquad (17.1c)$$

as in Chapters 1 (Volume I) and 8 (Volume II). This holds whatever hypothesis j is true. This identification of the d^3 matrix with a random choice between d^1 and d^2 is another aspect of the assumption that the choice of strategy does not affect the nature of the world. But we will see in a later section that this assumption can fail in Type B games, as defined in Chapter 8.

Again, here as in Chapters 1 and 8, outcomes must be defined such that the RDMs' preferences between probability distributions of outcomes depend on the probabilities themselves and not on how they are generated. In particular, if generating an outcome one way is more fun than generating it another way, and this influences choice, then the fun of the game is part of the outcome. One must also consider the fact that some probability distributions are themselves more fun than others. Lotteries, for example, are devoid of much of the excitement of the gambling process associated with, e.g., standing in a crowd around a craps table watching a fashionably dressed woman roll dice, or—for me, the ultimate rush— standing in a roaring crowd, cheering the horse you bet on for this race.

Nevertheless, lotteries are a form of entertainment and are quite profitable to the many states that hold them. More generally, the business of providing controlled risk is an enormous part of the world's economy, both legal and illegal. Think not only of lotteries and casinos; think also of suspenseful books and movies. Even romantic comedies must have moments when the eventual lovers' reconciliation seems seriously in doubt, even though one is absolutely sure that true love will prevail, or that the cowboy is not really blown to bits in the dynamite shed where the villains have locked him at the end of Episode 11 of a 15-episode serial movie that they used to show in Saturday matinees when I was a kid.

EXAMPLES

If there are m = 3 possible outcomes and n = 4 possible models of the world, then a decision is characterized by a matrix such as.

$$d = \begin{bmatrix} \frac{1}{2} & 0 & \frac{1}{3} & 0 \\ \frac{1}{4} & 1 & \frac{1}{3} & \frac{1}{2} \\ \frac{1}{4} & 0 & \frac{1}{3} & \frac{1}{2} \end{bmatrix}$$

If the strategy that provides this matrix is followed, and if the third possible nature of the world is true, then each possible outcome is equally likely. A decision that inevitably results in Outcome 1 has the matrix

$$e_1 = \begin{bmatrix} 1 & 1 & 1 & 1 \\ 0 & 0 & 0 & 0 \\ 0 & 0 & 0 & 0 \end{bmatrix}$$

A decision that gives probabilities ¼, ½, and ¼, respectively, to the three outcomes, whatever model is true, is

$$d = \begin{bmatrix} \frac{1}{4} & \frac{1}{4} & \frac{1}{4} & \frac{1}{4} \\ \frac{1}{2} & \frac{1}{2} & \frac{1}{2} & \frac{1}{2} \\ \frac{1}{4} & \frac{1}{4} & \frac{1}{4} & \frac{1}{4} \end{bmatrix}$$

This equals

$$d = \frac{1}{4}\begin{bmatrix} 1 & 1 & 1 & 1 \\ 0 & 0 & 0 & 0 \\ 0 & 0 & 0 & 0 \end{bmatrix} + \frac{1}{2}\begin{bmatrix} 0 & 0 & 0 & 0 \\ 1 & 1 & 1 & 1 \\ 0 & 0 & 0 & 0 \end{bmatrix} + \frac{1}{4}\begin{bmatrix} 0 & 0 & 0 & 0 \\ 0 & 0 & 0 & 0 \\ 1 & 1 & 1 & 1 \end{bmatrix}$$

The following matrix decision yields Outcome 1 if Hypothesis 1 is correct and Outcome 2 if otherwise:

$$d = \begin{pmatrix} 1 & 0 & 0 & 0 \\ 0 & 1 & 1 & 1 \\ 0 & 0 & 0 & 0 \end{pmatrix}$$

"OBJECTIVE" PROBABILITY

Savage (1954), page 67, conjectures that subjective probability is "the only probability concept essential to science and other activities that call upon probability." Other Bayesians contend that the concept of "objective probability" is meaningless, since any attempt to define it must be circular, defining the probability of one kind of event in terms of the probability of another. Since the concept is an integral part of the M59 IGA, I must explain what "objective probability" means in the M59 IGA and defend its usefulness. In particular, I have to explain what it *means* for an event to have, e.g., an "objective" 0.2 probability of occurring. I will discuss this in a later section of this chapter. Meanwhile, I *assume* that hypotheses involving objective probabilities are meaningful.

THE FORMAL M59 MODEL

In any specific application of M59, decisions and possible models of the world must be defined so that the choice of a decision does not alter "the world." For example, if it is possible that an RDM's purchase or sale of a security would alter its price, then hypotheses can be stated in terms of future prices. Otherwise, possible models-of-the-world would have to be stated in terms of supply-and-demand curves.

In order to comply with modern Rules of Inference as laid down and illustrated in Hilbert (1971, 1899), one must carefully distinguish between a "formal model" and its IGA (Intended General Application). For example, formally the fact that m is a positive integer is part of the M59 definition. The assertion that it is the number of possible outcomes, one and only one of which will happen, is part of M59's IGA. I cannot dispute Hilbert on this basic philosophical principle, but any attempt to continue to systematically distinguish M59 from its IGA would produce a pedantic mess and so will not be attempted.

A specific application of M59 assigns values to the following parameters:

$m > 0$	The number of possible outcomes, one and only one of which will occur
$n > 0$	The number of possible models of the world, one and only one of which is true
D	The set of all $m \times n$ matrices whose entries are nonnegative and whose columns each sum to one
$\{\} \geq \{\}$	A relationship among $d \in D$, i.e., given d^1 and $d^2 \in D$, the relationship is either true or false.

Definitions:

   $d^1 \sim d^2$ means $\{d^1\} \geq \{d^2\}$ *and* $\{d^2\} \geq \{d^1\}$

   $\{d^1\} > \{d^2\}$ means $\{d^1\} \geq \{d^2\}$ and *not* $\{d^2\} \geq (d^1)$

For every h in [1, m], let

   $e_h = (p_{ij})$ such that

   $p_{hj} = 1$ for $j = h$

   $p_{ij} = 0$, otherwise clearly

   $e_h \in D$

Axiom I

(a) For any two matrices, d^1 and d^2 in D, either $\{d^1\} \geq \{d^2\}$ or
     $\{d^2\} \geq \{d^1\}$ (or both).

(b) If $\{d^1\} \geq \{d^2\}$ and $\{d^2\} \geq \{d^3\}$, then $\{d^1\} \geq \{d^3\}$.

(c) There are i_1 and i_0 such that $\{e_{i_1}\} > \{e_{i_0}\}$.

Axiom II

For any d^1, d^2, d^3 in D: If $\{d^1\} > \{d^2\}$, then $\{pd^1 + (1 - p)\, d^3\} >$
$\{pd^2 + (1 - p)\, d^3\}$ for any $p \in (0,1)$.

Axiom III

If d^1, d^2 and d^3 are in D, and if $\{d^1\} > \{d^2\} > \{d^3\}$, then there
exists a $p \in (0,1)$ such that $d^2 \sim pd^1 + (1 - p)\, d^3$.

   By definition, the probability distribution P^1 is at least as
good as P^2, written $\{P^1\} \geq \{P^2\}$, if the decision matrix, d^1, each

of whose columns equals P^1, is at least as good as the decision matrix, d^2, each of whose columns equals P^2.

E.g.,

$$\left\{\begin{matrix} \tfrac{1}{4} \\ \tfrac{1}{2} \\ \tfrac{1}{4} \end{matrix}\right\} \geq \left\{\begin{matrix} \tfrac{1}{3} \\ \tfrac{1}{3} \\ \tfrac{1}{3} \end{matrix}\right\}$$

means, by definition, that

$$\left\{\begin{matrix} \tfrac{1}{4} & \tfrac{1}{4} & \tfrac{1}{4} & \tfrac{1}{4} \\ \tfrac{1}{2} & \tfrac{1}{2} & \tfrac{1}{2} & \tfrac{1}{2} \\ \tfrac{1}{4} & \tfrac{1}{4} & \tfrac{1}{4} & \tfrac{1}{4} \end{matrix}\right\} \geq \left\{\begin{matrix} \tfrac{1}{3} & \tfrac{1}{3} & \tfrac{1}{3} & \tfrac{1}{3} \\ \tfrac{1}{3} & \tfrac{1}{3} & \tfrac{1}{3} & \tfrac{1}{3} \\ \tfrac{1}{3} & \tfrac{1}{3} & \tfrac{1}{3} & \tfrac{1}{3} \end{matrix}\right\}$$

This definition is required, since M59 does not otherwise define an ordering of probability vectors.

Axiom IV

Let P_j^1 and P_j^2 be the jth columns of d^1 and d^2, respectively; then if $\{P_j^1\} \geq \{P_j^2\}$ for every j, then $\{d^1\} \geq \{d^2\}$.

In Words

Axiom I, Parts (a) and (b), says that the RDM's preferences constitute a simple linear ordering of the d ∈ D matrices. Part (c) says that not all outcomes are equally preferred. If one drops Part (c), expected utility still holds, trivially, but probability beliefs become irrelevant and indeterminate.

Axiom II is the "coin flipping" or "coffee without milk versus coffee without cream" axiom discussed in Chapter 1 (in Volume I).

Axiom III is the continuity axiom, also discussed in Chapter 1. In particular, Chapter 1 notes an alternative version of Axiom III that is perhaps more "self-evident," and perhaps makes clearer the nature of the continuity assumption, but has a more complex definition.

Axiom IV says that if—no matter what hypothesis about the world is true—Decision 1 is at least as preferred as Decision 2, then Decision 1 is at least as preferred as Decision 2. I have borrowed the "sure thing" phrase principle from Savage (1954) to characterize Axiom IV, although the meaning is somewhat different here than there. Surely, in the context of M59, a strategy that is at least as preferred as another—no matter what the nature of the world—must epitomize what is meant by a "sure thing."

Comment on Axiom I

Axiom I requires the RDM to have no fuzziness in the perception of its preferences. In particular,

> if A is exactly as preferred as B,
>
> and B is exactly as preferred as C,
>
> . . .
>
> and Y is exactly as preferred as Z,
>
> THEN A is exactly as preferred as Z.

Part (c) rules a thoroughly boring case.

It is important to realize how little Axiom I requires of an ordering of the $d \in D$ and, consequently, how much the remaining three axioms must bring to the party to characterize the M59 IGA. By way of illustration, suppose that the P_{ij}^d of every decision matrix, d, had to be a multiple of 0.01. In that case D would consist of a finite though humongous number, M, of different d-matrices. Imagine each of these d-matrices printed on a giant playing card. Then D would be a deck of such cards. Shuffle D. Write numbers 1 through M on the cards in the order the cards appear in this randomized deck. A preference ordering according to this random ordering would satisfy Axiom I. The job of the remaining three axioms is to restrict the set of possible orderings of $d \in D$ to the intended interpretation of the rows, columns and entries of the d-matrices and the matrices themselves.

Comment on Axiom II

Axiom II says that if Strategy 1 is better than Strategy 2, then a chance of Strategy 1 versus Strategy 3 is better than the same chance of Strategy 2 versus Strategy 3. Markowitz (1959), page 263, illustrates the axiom by a mythical example, namely

> *The Keeper of Strategies has selected three large books, each containing a complete strategy that tells what to buy and sell under specific circumstances at various times. Our RDM has inspected each of these*

volumes and has decided that it prefers Strategy 1 to Strategy 2. The Keeper of Strategies announces that it will spin a wheel with probability p of generating a One, and probability (1 – p) of generating a Zero. If One appears, then Strategy 3 must be followed. If Zero appears, then the RDM has its choice of Strategy 1 or Strategy 2.

The RDM is required to state in advance which it will choose. Our axiom asserts that the RDM will choose Strategy 1 rather than Strategy 2 if the opportunity arises, whatever the Strategy 3 that it does not get and the probability p with which it did not get it.

The M59 Axiom I (simple ordering) and Axiom II (the coin-tossing axiom) imply that "randomization *never* adds value." On the other hand, there are situations in which randomization clearly *does* add value. Examples include the design of agricultural experiments, the use of Nash symmetry (see Chapter 10 in Volume II) when, for example, a coin is flipped at the start of a football game to determine which side gets to choose whether to "kick" or "receive" first, and "mixed strategies" in the von Neumann and Morgenstern (1944) zero-sum two-person game.

Ellsberg (1961) presents experimental situations in which, after careful consideration, many subjects prefer randomization. Later sections of this chapter address these issues.

Axiom System M59X, discussed later in this chapter, explores the consequences of dropping Axiom III. Axiom IV needs no defense in a system that seeks rational behavior in the face of Knightian uncertainty.

INITIAL CONSEQUENCES

As shown in Chapter 12 of Markowitz (1959), if an RDM acts according to the preceding four axioms, it also acts according to the expected utility/personal probability (EU/PB) rule: namely, there are numbers $u_1, \ldots, u_m$ and $\pi_1, \ldots \pi_n$, where the π_j are nonnegative and sum to one such that decision matrices $d = (p_{ij})$ are ordered by

$$EU = \sum_j \pi_j \left(\sum_i p_{ij} u_i \right)$$

(17.2a)

or, in matrix notation,

$$EU = (u_1, \ldots, u_m)(p_{ij}) \begin{bmatrix} \pi_1 \\ \cdot \\ \cdot \\ \cdot \\ \pi_n \end{bmatrix}$$

(17.2b)

By convention, the π_j are nonnegative, unique and sum to one, whereas the u_i are unique up to an increasing linear transformation. I say "by convention" since the origin and scaling of either or both the π and the u is arbitrary. I require

$$\pi_j \geq 0 \quad j = 1, \ldots, n$$

$$\sum_{j=1}^{n} \pi_j = 1$$

(17.2c)

and *interpret* $\pi_i = 0$ to mean that there is no "finite" chance that the hypothesis is true. ("Infinitesimal π_j" is discussed later.)

Later sections of this chapter will define, defend and illustrate the Markowitz (1959) Chapter 12 assertion that—for an RDM following the axioms of M59—"subjective probabilities" (i.e., the π_j) and any "objective probability" information that the RDM may have concerning which of the n hypotheses is true "mix on a par." In particular, the RDM following M59 is indifferent between a bet at given *objective* odds and the same bet in which the RDM assigns the same *subjective* odds to the outcomes. Clearly, the plausibility of this implication of the M59 and M59X axiom systems must be examined.

BAYES'S RULE

The fundamental tenets of Bayesianism are that one should observe the following rules:

A. Assign probability beliefs where objective probabilities are not known, and

B. Update these beliefs according to Bayes's rule as observations accumulate.

Some would say that there is no such thing as "objective probabilities," but Rule (A) implicitly covers that case. Rule (B) follows from Rule (A). In particular, for finite probability spaces, Bayes's rule says that

$$P(H_i \mid O) = P(H_i)\, P(O \mid H_i) / \sum_{j=1}^{n} P(H_j) P(O|H_j) \quad (17.3)$$

where $P(H_i)$ is the prior belief in H_i, $P(O|H_i)$ is the objective probability of observing O if H_i is true, and $P(H_i|O)$ is the posterior belief in H_i given Observation O.

Because subjective and objective probabilities "mix on a par" for an M59 RDM, Bayes's Rule (B) is covered by the section on "The Solution of Type A Games" in Chapter 8 (in Volume II). Specifically, Equation (17.3) is the conditional probability (subjective, as it happens) that H_i is true, given that O is observed.

A BAYESIAN VIEW OF MVA

MVA (mean-variance analysis) requires estimates of means, variances and covariances. Theoretically, these should be forward-looking estimates. Even if one wanted to avoid any subjectivity in one's portfolio analysis by basing estimates strictly on historical returns without any subjective input, the choice of historical period greatly alters estimates and is thus, itself, a subjective forward-looking decision. Thus, inevitably—explicitly or implicitly—MVA in practice is based on the probability beliefs of some analyst or team or the accident of when published time series began.

Consider, for example, the case treated in Chapters 2, 3 and 4 (in Volume I), namely, that of an RDM who seeks to maximize the expected value, E(U(R)), of a concave function of single-period return—except that now probabilities include the subjective probabilities, π_j, that the RDM (individual or team) attaches to hypotheses about the world, as well as the objective probabilities, P_{ij}^d, that the outcome O_i will occur if hypothesis j is true and a particular decision, d, is chosen. In the present case, the O_i are levels of portfolio return R_i. According to Equation 8.12 (i.e., Equation 12 in Chapter 8 of Volume II),

$$EU = E(E(U|h_j))$$

$$= \sum_{j=1}^{n} \pi_j \left(\sum_{i=1}^{m} p_{ij} u_i \right) \tag{17.4a}$$

where

$$U_i = U(R_i) \tag{17.4b}$$

is the utility of the ith level of return. A mean-variance approximation to EU would be a function of the mean and variance of this partly objective, partly subjective probability distribution of portfolio return which, itself, in turn, is the familiar linear and quadratic functions of the means, variances and covariances of investment returns. The latter—means, variances and covariances of investment returns—depend on the moments of the RDM's subjective beliefs as well as hypothesized objective probabilities. Specifically, let μ_j and V_j be the forecast mean and variance of some asset's return for the time-interval of the MVA given that hypothesis j is true. Then Equation 8.12 implies that the RDM's expected return for this asset is

$$E(R) = \sum_{j=1}^{N} \pi_j \mu_j \qquad (17.5)$$

Thus, plausibly enough, the expected return that the RDM estimates for a security (or asset class or portfolio) is the average overall hypotheses of the expected returns given these hypotheses, weighted by the probabilities that the RDM assigns to each hypothesis.

The formula for the RDM's variance of estimate is less obvious. It may be derived as follows:

$E((R - E(R))^2|h_j)$

$= E((R - \mu j + \mu j - E(R))^2|h_j)$

$= E(((R - \mu_j)^2 + (\mu_j - E(R))^2 + 2(R - \mu_j)(\mu_j - E(R)))|h_j)$

$= E((R - \mu_j)^2|h_j) + E((\mu_j - E(R))^2|h_j + 2E((R - \mu_j)(\mu_j - E(R))|h_j)$

$= V_j + E((\mu_j - E(R))^2|h_j) \qquad (17.6a)$

The last term is zero, since for any given j,

$$E((R - \mu_j|j_j) = 0 \qquad (17.6b)$$

Thus

$$V(R) = E((R - E(R))^2 = E(E((R - E(R))^2|H) = E(V) + V(\mu)$$
$$(17.7a)$$

The first term on the right is the average variance

$$E(V_j) = \sum_{j=1}^{N} \pi_j V_j$$
$$(17.7b)$$

It is comparable to the formula for $E(R)$ shown in Equation Equation (17.5). The second term on the right is the variance of μ,

$$V(\mu) = E[\mu - E(R)]^2 \qquad (17.7c)$$

This is the subjective variance which the RDM ascribes to its estimate of μ.

Therefore, the variance the RDM's estimate of the return to an investment reflects not only the *subjective mean of the objective variances* but also the *subjective variance of the objective means*. As shown in endnote[2], a comparable relationship holds for the Bayesian RDM's estimate of the covariance between the returns, R_i and R_j, of two securities.

JUDGMENT, APPROXIMATION AND AXIOM III

Axiom III is a continuity, or "Archimedean," axiom. The consequences of omitting the Archimedean axiom from axiom systems such as M59 have been thoroughly explored, for both finite and nonfinite models and for the "risk" and the "uncertainty" cases. In particular, it is analyzed in back-to-back articles by Melvin Hausner (1952) and R. M. Thrall (1954). Hausner says that his and Thrall's articles are based on research done at the RAND Corporation by Thrall and Norman Dalkey. (Small world: Markowitz [1959] acknowledges beneficial conversations with Norman Dalkey related to his exploration of alternative axiom systems in Chapters 10, 11, 12 and Appendix C of that work.) Further development, principally for nonfinite cases and for both Knightian risk and Knightian uncertainty, are in Chipman et al. (1990) and Fishburn (1970).

The principal implication for M59 of this research is that if Axiom III is dropped but Axioms I, II and IV are retained, then the RDM orders decisions "lexicographically." Consider, first, the case with known odds. If Axiom III is omitted from M59, then the remaining axioms imply that an RDM would assign to each decision a (perhaps) multidimensional utility vector

$$U = (U^1, U^2, \ldots, U^K) \tag{17.8}$$

for

$$1 \leq K \leq K$$

These utility vectors are ordered lexicographically, like the entries in the dictionary, i.e., if

$$U^1 \succcurlyeq V^1 \tag{17.9a}$$

then $\{U\} > \{V\}$. If $U^1 = U^2$, then U^2 and V^2 are compared. In particular, if

$$U^1 = V^1 \quad \text{and} \quad U^2 > V^2 \tag{17.9b}$$

then

$$\{U\} > \{V\} \tag{17.9c}$$

Strictly speaking, it is the probability distribution, P, to which U is associated that is preferred over the Q to which V is associated, but I will continue to speak of preferences as applied to U and V as well as to probability distributions P and Q. Generally,

$$\{ U \} > \{ V \} \tag{17.9d}$$

$$\text{If } U^k > V^k$$
$$\text{for some } 1 \le k \le K$$
$$\text{and}$$
$$U_j = V_j$$
$$\text{for all } j < k \tag{17.10}$$

The dimensionality, K, of the utility vector in Equation (17.8) depends on the RDM's preferences. If $K = 1$, a single utility is attached to each d-matrix, and the Archimedean axiom holds. Dropping the Archimedean axiom does not *pre-clude* it from holding in any particular application. It just does not *require* it to do so.

In Chapter 1 of this book (in Volume I), I argued that the Archimedean axiom is applicable to single-period portfolio returns. For example, **IF** there were **no** probability, p, of a 100% loss versus breaking even that was as good as a 99% loss *with certainty*, then the RDM would prefer the certainty of a sure 99% loss to the virtual certainty (say, a p = 0.99999 chance) of breaking even versus the slightest (1 − p) chance of a 100% loss. Personally, I would not want my RDM to act that way on my behalf. The same argument applies for the certainty of R = −0.98 as opposed to R = −0.99, etc.

The analysis in Chapter 1 is fine as far as it goes, but MVA seeks mean-variance efficiency subject to constraints. *Why constraints?* In particular, how do constraints relate to the "Portfolio Selection context," which is the subject of Chapter 6 (in Volume II)? *Perhaps* they reflect overriding goals other than the accumulation of wealth.

In the uncertainty case, absent the Archimedean Axiom, the π_i's too may be vectors ordered lexicographically. For example, what probability should physicists have placed before 1900 on the proposition that Newton's universal law of gravity is wrong? It seems to me that the probability should have been a nonzero infinitesimal.

As noted in Chapter 10 (in Volume II), George Dantzig (1951, 1963) used powers of hypothetical epsilon constant,

ϵ, to break ties. Specifically, the ith power of epsilon, ϵ^i, was added to the ith constraint equation. The comparisons would involve two or more X_i's going to zero at the same time. The comparison, then, would be between *polynomials* in ϵ. The existence of a winner was assured by the nonsingularity of the basis matrix which ensured a unique winner. Markowitz (1959) uses the same methodology to resolve ties with the X_i and/or μ_j.

To put it bluntly, Abraham Robinson "discovered" infinitesimals in 1974, but my mentor, George Dantzig, figured out how to use these wee creatures circa 1951.

(1) A PHILOSOPHICAL DIFFERENCE BETWEEN S54 AND M59

There are two principal differences between M59 and S54.

1. M59 assumes that there are only a finite number of outcomes and hypotheses; S54 is more general.
2. In M59 **if** a particular hypothesis is true, **then** there is an "objective" probability distribution of possible outcomes. In contrast, the concept of objective probability is avoided in S54.

Concerning Limitation (1), the payoff from our study of Cantor, Skolem, Peano and such concerns the Peano principle of mathematical induction:

If Proposition P(1) is true, and

If P(i) is true implies P(i + 1) is true,

Then P(i) is true for all i

This is usually thought of as applying to finite i. But there is nothing that says that it *cannot* apply as well to transfinite i. Thus, the N in Markowitz (1959) may be viewed as any "ordinal number," finite or transfinite.

Concerning the second difference between S54 and M59, as a matter of principle, S54 admits *no* "objective" probabilities. Specifically, on page 56 of Savage (1954), the author says:

It is my tentative view that the concept of personal probability introduced and illustrated in the preceding chapter is, except possibly for slight modifications, the only probability concept essential to science and other activities that call upon probability.

Some Bayesians hold an even more extreme view—that objective probability is *meaningless*, since any attempt at a definition of probability is inevitably in terms of some disguised version of probability.

Savage (1954), page 3, distinguishes

. . . three main classes of views on the interpretation of probability, for the purposes of this book, calling them objectivistic, personalistic, and necessary.

Objectivistic views hold that some repetitive events, such as tosses of a penny, prove to be in reasonably close agreement with the mathematical concept of independently repeated random events, all with the same probability. According to such views, evidence for the quality of agreement between the behavior of the repetitive event and the mathematical concept, and for the magnitude of the probability that applies (in case any does), is to be obtained by observation of some repetitions of the event, and from no other source whatsoever.

Personalistic views hold that probability measures the confidence that a particular individual has in the truth of a particular proposition, for example, the proposition that it will rain tomorrow. These views postulate that the individual concerned is in some ways "reasonable," but they do not deny the possibility that two reasonable individuals faced with the same evidence may have different degrees of confidence in the truth of the same proposition.

Necessary views hold that probability measures the extent to which one set of propositions, out of logical necessity and apart from human opinion, confirms the truth of another. They are generally regarded by their holders as extensions of logic, which tells when one set of propositions necessitates the truth of another.

The "necessary" view of probability is not currently a major contender for the hearts and minds of practicing statisticians. Since there is quite a bit that needs to be said about "objectivistic" versus "personalistic" views, I will not discuss the necessary view, except to note that the most famous proponent of this view is John Maynard Keynes (2008, 1920).

On page 4 of his 1954 book, Savage further comments:

The difficulty in the objectivistic position is this. In any objectivistic view, probabilities can apply fruitfully only to repetitive events, that is, to certain processes; and (depending on the view in question) it is either meaningless to talk about the probability that a given proposition is true, or this probability can be only 1 or 0, according as the proposition is in fact true or false. Under neither interpretation can probability serve as a measure of the trust to be put in the proposition. Thus the existence of evidence for a proposition can never, on an objectivistic view, be expressed by saying that the proposition is true with a certain probability. Again, if one must choose among several courses of action in the light of experimental evidence, it is not meaningful, in terms of objective probability, to compute which of these actions is most promising, that is, which has the highest expected income. Holders of objectivistic views have, therefore, no recourse but to argue that it is not reasonable to assign probabilities to the truth of propositions or to calculate which of several actions is the most promising, and that the need expressed by the attempt to set up such concepts must be met in other ways, if at all.

I view Savage's classification of "views on the interpretation of probability" as deficient. In particular, it does not admit my own choice of views, namely that of *subjective* probabilities concerning which *objective* probability distribution is true for a given situation. Here we have an example of a proposition about a proposition, namely a subjective proposition (the probability of something being true) about an objective proposition, i.e., the probability distribution of outcomes.

The next two sections explore the concepts of truly "objective" probabilities and "propositions about propositions."

EXAMPLES OF CLEARLY "OBJECTIVE" PROBABILITIES

Three examples should suffice to illustrate the importance of randomness in the physical sciences and the nuisance it would be to state propositions in terms of beliefs about objects rather than the objects themselves.

1. *The Diffusion Equation.* The IGA of the diffusion equation was the possible time-paths of (e.g.) one liquid introduced into another. The Black-Scholes Option Pricing Model is a non-IGA application of the diffusion equation. The objects hypothesized to have

random motion are molecules in one application and stock prices in the other. The hypothesis in each case is that the object moved according to these stochastic laws, not that someone's belief changed according to them.

2. *Entropy.* If two chambers, one with a vacuum and the other containing a gas under pressure, are separated by a partition, and the partition is removed, molecules from the chamber with the greater pressure will give molecules to that with the lesser pressure until the two chambers have equal pressure on their walls. The movement from a more "organized" system—with much greater pressure in one place and much less in another—to a less organized one, with approximately equal pressure everywhere, is referred to as an "increase in entropy." Statistical mechanics hypothesizes that this macro phenomenon is due to the "random" collisions of countless molecules, some of which are bouncing off the walls of Container B, and others are encountering no such wall where the partition has been removed.

   The statistical mechanical hypothesis is concerned with probabilities of the speed and direction of the objects considered rather than about anyone's belief about these many particular molecules.

3. *Max Born's "Probability Waves."* Einstein famously wrote, in a letter to Max Born, that "[t]he theory says a lot, but does not really bring us any closer to the

secret of the 'old one.' I, at any rate, am convinced
that He is not playing at dice."

Max Born was Werner Heisenberg's professor and
the one who hypothesized that the waves described by
Schrodinger's equation are "probability waves."

The last example illustrates a danger in viewing inferences concerning deterministic hypotheses and inferences
concerning statistical hypotheses as two completely different
things; since one of the great physicists in this interchange
was sure that a deterministic hypothesis must be an ultimate
explanation, whereas the other was satisfied with the stochastic hypothesis.

PROPOSITIONS ABOUT PROPOSITIONS

Various types of entities are involved in discussions about
subjective and objective probability. Some of these entities are
propositions, namely statements that are either true or false.
Some such propositions are either *always* true or *always* false.
These are either definitions, axioms or theorems that follow
logically from the former two. Finally, a word sequence not
capable of being either true or false is potentially a testable
hypothesis. For this a mapping must be made between implications of some set of propositions taken together and kind of
observation.

Some statements are of the SVO form, namely "Subject
Verb Object."

It follows from the preceding paragraph that the "object" itself may be a proposition. Examples include

Paul thinks that the dice are fair.
Mary thinks that the dice are loaded.
John thinks that a 7 or 11 will appear on the next roll.
Wikipedia says that the half-life of carbon-14 is 5,730
    years ± 40 years.

Statements of this type are central to a discussion of subjective versus objective probability. In the examples, Paul, Mary and John are the "subjects." What they think is "subjective" and, in fact, varies from one to the other. In general, a subjective belief is a proposition about another proposition. For example, "Paul thinks that the dice are fair" is a proposition about Paul concerning a proposition about the dice. Mary's statement is a proposition about the same dice. One can also have propositions about propositions about propositions. An example would be Harry thinks that Aristotle would say that the dice in question are *either* fair *or not* fair. The passage cited from the Wikipedia article about carbon-14's half-life is a statement about carbon-14—not, in itself, a statement about what anyone thinks about carbon-14. It is, of course the object of the statement that "Wikipedia says that. . . . "

A PROBLEM WITH AXIOM II

So much for the analysis of "he said that I said that you said that she said" propositions. Now back to the critique of the Axioms.

Axiom II may be interpreted *either* as a statement about a one-period game in which the decision-maker makes a choice at Time-Point Zero and receives its payoff at Time-Point One. *Or*, Axiom II may be interpreted as a statement about the normal form of a many-period game as discussed in Chapter 8 (in Volume II). The two views must have the same optimum strategy for the same game. Thus, Axiom II is tautological, therefore irrefutable. Axioms I and II together imply that randomization never adds value. But: in von Neumann's two-person game each player typically plays a "mixed," i.e., randomized, strategy; football games start with a flip of a coin; and biological experiments randomize. *What gives?*

1. Game Theory

We saw in Chapter 8 (Volume 2) that von Neumann and Morgenstern (1944) recommend "mixed strategies" for, e.g., the zero-sum two-person game. For example, one can assure oneself of equal probabilities of a win, lose or draw in any play of "rock, paper, scissors" (RPS) by making one's own choice randomly.

Axiom II is concerned with the choice between probability distributions of outcomes given various hypotheses. The outcome of the RPS game is either win, lose or draw. Presumably, each player would prefer to win than to lose. To see why Axiom

II is inapplicable to such a von Neumann and Morgenstern two-person zero-sum game, consider the decision matrices, d $= (p_{ij})$, whose columns represent strategies that one's opponent might adopt or abilities the opponent might have. Specifically, suppose that *one* hypothesis is that the opponent randomizes, and the other is that the opponent will try to guess one's move, and differ in their estimate of one's opponent's ability to out-guess you if you don't randomize. Suppose further that a play of the game consists of RPS moves until someone wins, i.e., in case of ties, try again. (As in the craps game in Chapter 8 [in Volume II], let's ignore the possibility that a "move" of the game would go on practically forever.) Further suppose that we represent the d-matrix of any strategy as in Exhibit 17.2, with the two rows (outcomes) labeled W for "win" and L for "lose."

EXHIBIT 17.2 Decision Matrices for a Hypothetical Game

R		Relative Skill Levels					
W	½	1.0	0.8	0.6	0.4	0.2	0.0
L	½	0.0	0.2	0.4	0.6	0.8	1.0

(a) The d^N matrix

	R		Relative Skill Levels				
W	½	½	½	½	½	½	½
L	½	½	½	½	½	½	½

(b) The d^R matrix

The contents of the d-matrices, here as in general, depend on the strategy one adopts. In particular, Exhibit (17.2b) represents the results of one randomizing. Whatever the opponent's strategy, one has a 50-50 chance of a win or a loss. Exhibit 17.2a on the other hand, could represent the probability of a win as a function of our own and our opponent's relative skill levels. For example, consider the following three strategies:

A. Play "rock" on the first move; then thereafter randomize if the play of the game is not over.
B. Play "paper" on the first move; then randomize thereafter if the game is not over after the first move.
C. Play "scissor" on the first move; and then randomize.

In all these cases, randomization is used because any attempt to outguess in a systemic game opens the possibility that our opponent will outguess us. If one randomizes between Strategies (A), (B) and (C), then every move has been randomized.

2. Fairness

A coin is flipped at the beginning of a football game to decide who will get their choice as to whether to "kick" or "receive" at the start of the game. This is an example of a social choice that is resolved by a Nash-symmetric procedure, as described in Chapter 10 (in Volume II).

3. Experimental Design

In his famous book, *The Design of Experiments* (1935), R. A. Fisher describes (or prescribes) how "treatments" of crops are to be randomly assigned to plots of land. The result neverthe-less may be idiosyncratic since the year may differ in one or another way from all other years.

In each of these cases, the generally accepted correct pro-cedure violates Axiom II.

ARE THE π_j PROBABILITIES
THE SCALING OF THE π_j?

The characterization of the π_i as subjective probabilities relies on the scaling of the π_j in Equation (17.11) to be nonnegative and sum to one. But alternative scalings of the u_i and π_j would give the same rankings. For example, the π_j can be multiplied by a positive constant

$$\tilde{\pi}_j = \beta\tilde{\pi}_j \qquad \beta > 0 \qquad\qquad (17.11a)$$

without altering the rankings specified by Equation (17.2). If u_j were scaled to sum to one

$$\Sigma\tilde{u} = 1 \qquad\qquad (17.11b)$$

then any positive linear transformation of the $\tilde{\pi}$

$$\tilde{\pi}_j = \alpha + \beta\tilde{\pi}_j \qquad \beta > 0 \qquad\qquad (17.11c)$$

would give the same ranking as Equation (17.2). This raises a question, not addressed in Markowitz (1959), as to whether there is some justification for the scaling used in Equation (17.3), other than a desire to provide an axiomatic justification for the use of the Bayes rule.

In Chapter 10 (in Volume II), in a quite different context, it seemed "natural" to scale utility so that the best alternative had utility 1.0 and the worst had utility 0.0. By "natural" I mean that when we scale utility that way, we implicitly assume that the reader concurs that a reasonable way to normalize the utility scale is to let $U = 1$ be the best outcome and $U = 0$ the worst, and other utility levels therefore represent a fraction of the utility-distance between best and worst.

To adopt the same convention here, if we let

$$u(e_{i1}) = 1.0 \qquad\qquad (17.12a)$$
$$u(e_{i0}) = 1.0 \qquad\qquad (17.12b)$$

Then $u(e_i)$ for each other e_i equals the probability, p, such that

$$e_i : pe_{i1} + (1 - p)e_{i0} \qquad\qquad (17.12c)$$

Then the π_j are equal to the probability, g_j, such that

$$g_j : qe_{i1} + (1 - q)e_{i0} \qquad\qquad (17.12d)$$

The best possible decision yields $U = 1$ with certainty, and the worst possible decision yields $U = 0$, with certainty. With such conventions $\pi_j \geq 0$, else Equation (17.3) could rank that decision worse than e_{i0}; and $\sum \pi_j = 1$ is required, else a combination of bets could rank higher than e_{i1}.

THE π_j "MIX ON A PAR" WITH OBJECTIVE PROBABILITIES

Markowitz (1959) Chapter 12 shows that the $d \in D$ of an RDM following the preceding axioms can be ordered by their vectors of utilities $V = (U_1, \ldots, U_n)$, where U_j is the expected utility associated with a decision if the jth model is true. In particular, if the RDM's choice is consistent with these axioms, then its ordering of the $d \in D$ can be described by a linear function like that in the preceding section:

$$V = \sum_j \pi_j U_j$$

where

$$\sum \pi_j = 1, \pi_j \geq 0 \qquad (17.13)$$

The present section continues to consider the justification for referring to the π_j as "probabilities." In particular, I will note or illustrate that

A. When objective probabilities are associated with hypotheses, the π_j equal these objective probabilities;

B. When some objective probabilities are known,
the subjective probabilities π_j and the objective
probabilities "mix on a par" with each other;

C. The subjective probabilities obey the same arithmetic
relationships as do objective probabilities; and

D. For an RDM choosing in accord with the four axioms
of M59, it is no more desirable to bet on objective
probabilities than on subjective ones.

Specifically, in interpreting the π_j here, I note cases in
which the same decision situation can be modeled in two different ways with M59 and require of course that the RDM's
choice must be the same whichever way *we* choose to model
the situation. I start with illustrative special cases and then
proceed to the general analysis.

The π_j Are the Objective Probabilities When the Latter Are Known

A. The analyses in Volumes I and II of this book with known
probability distributions imply that when *objective* probabilities are known for all contingencies, an RDM that follows these axioms maximizes expected utility. In particular,
since the "utilities" determined by the RDM's preferences are
unique except in terms of increasing linear transformation,
if objective probabilities are known for the various possible
models of the world, the weights in

$$V = \sum_j \pi_j U_j \qquad (17.14)$$

would be these objective probabilities.

Subjective and Objective Probabilities "Mix on a Par"

B1. Suppose that it was known that either model of the world, A, B, or C, is true. Suppose it was further known that if either B or C is true, there is a 50-50 chance that it is the former rather than the latter. Since there is no objective probability attached to A versus (B or C), we cannot attach an objective probability to either B or C individually. However, if subjective probabilities are to "mix on a par" with objective probabilities, we must have $\pi_A = \pi_B = (\tfrac{1}{2}) \pi_{(A\,or\,B)}$. Is this necessarily true for rational behavior following the four axioms?

The present situation is one that can be analyzed in two different ways: On the one hand, we can say that there are three possible models, A, B, and C, and that each decision is characterized by three probability distributions, P_A, P_B, P_C. Or, on the other hand, we could say that there are two models of the world, A and D, where D represents there being a 50-50 chance of B or C being true. In the latter form of analysis, each decision is represented by two distributions, P_A and P_D, where

$$P_D = (\tfrac{1}{2}) P_B + (\tfrac{1}{2}) P_C.$$

Since an RDM's preferences clearly do not depend on how we analyze the situation, the π_A, π_B, or π_C of any particular

RDM must be such as to produce the same orderings in both modes of analysis.

Specifically,

$$
\begin{aligned}
V &= \pi_A U_A + \pi_D U_D \\
&= \pi_A U_A + \pi_D [(\tfrac{1}{2})U_B + (\tfrac{1}{2})U_C] \\
&= \pi_A U_A + [(\tfrac{1}{2})\pi_D]U_B + (\tfrac{1}{2})\pi_D]U_C \\
&= \pi_A U_A + \pi_B U_B + \pi_C U_C \qquad\qquad (17.15)
\end{aligned}
$$

Therefore, we must have $\pi_B = \pi_C = \tfrac{1}{2}\pi_D$.

B2. A different kind of situation containing both objective and subjective probabilities is one in which there is a 50-50 chance that either A is true or that one element of (B or C) is true. However, no objective probabilities are known for B versus C given that (B or C) is true. In this case, if subjective and objective probabilities are to "mix on a par," we must have $\pi_B + \pi_C = \tfrac{1}{2}$. Suppose that if this were not so, then the utility

$$
V = \pi_A U_A + \pi_B U_B + \pi_C U_C
$$

attached to the utility vector (0, 1, 1) would not equal $\tfrac{1}{2}$. Therefore (0, 1, 1) would not be considered exactly as good as $(\tfrac{1}{2})(0,0,0) + (\tfrac{1}{2})(1,1,1)$. But this cannot be so, since both analyses represent the same objective probability distribution; since, by hypothesis, the decision (0, 1, 1) has a 50-50 chance of receiving $U = 1$, as does the decision $(\tfrac{1}{2})(0,0,0) + (\tfrac{1}{2})(1,1,1)$. Thus, the RDM must have

$$\pi_B + \pi_C = \frac{1}{2}$$

B3. Exhibit 17.1 illustrates yet another case, namely one in which the RDM knows a *conditional* probability of subset A given that subset B is true; i.e.,

$$P(A|B) = \frac{P(A \text{ and } B)}{P(B)} \qquad (17.16)$$

The argument that a strategy that provides a subjective conditional probability

$$P(A|B) = k$$

would have the same utility as an M59 RDM had the probabilities been objective, is essentially the same as the argument for unconditional probability in B2.

C. Suppose that there were three possible models of the world, A, B, and C. Suppose further that we are considering two decisions which have the same payoff if either Model A or Model B is true. Then

$$V = \pi_A U_A + \pi_B U_B + \pi_C U_C$$
$$= U_A(\pi_A + \pi_B) + \pi_C U_C \qquad (17.17)$$

If the π were objective probabilities, $\pi_A + \pi_B$ would be the probability that either A or B is true. But, as illustrated in Equation (17.16), this interpretation is satisfied in the case of subjective probabilities as well. In general, we may define the probability of a set of possible mutually exclusive models to be the sum of their probabilities. Whenever utility is the same for all members of the set, we may say that a utility is attached to the statement "one of the models in this set is true," and we may multiply this utility by the "probability of the set" D. In short, the π_j combine by the same rules as objective probability, and they mix with objective probabilities without any "haircut" for being subjective rather than objective.

An M59 RDM considers it no more desirable to bet on objective than subjective probabilities!

That is a strong conclusion. You can either accept it or reject, e.g., the coin-flipping axiom. A third choice is that accepting the objective is "infinitesimally" better than a subjective one with the same odds; i.e., the objective bet is preferred to the subjective one with the same odds but not to any subjective bet with higher odds, no matter how close the difference. This violates the continuity assumption. See the discussion of infinitesimals in Chapter 16.

18

INDUCTION PRACTICE

INTRODUCTION

This book's subtitle promises to discuss practice as well as theory. As explained in the two preceding volumes, and earlier in the present one, by "practice" I mean how an HDM could in fact approximate the behavior—and the results—of an RDM. In the preceding chapter, we saw that an RDM who acted according to a few plausible axioms would maximize expected utility (EU) using probability beliefs (PB) where objective probabilities are not known and would update these beliefs according to Bayes's rule. In practice, where are we to get these prior beliefs, or how are we to proceed without them? The remainder of this volume is principally devoted to this question. In particular, the present chapter considers

1. Objective procedures such as the R. A. Fisher (1960) tests of significance and the Neyman-Pearson (1933) hypothesis test;
2. Robust statistical procedures;

3. Bayesian analysis using "conjugate priors";

4. Resampling, boot strapping and empirical Bayes;

5. Graphical procedures; and

6. Bayes's factor (BF) regions.

These six types of procedures will not necessarily be discussed separately. Rather, the chapter should be thought of as one giant free-for-all wherein any individual or group gets to pile up on any other individual or group. No contestant emerges unscathed.

I assume that the results of a statistical analysis will be disseminated to HDMs who may take, or refrain from taking, important actions based on these results. Examples include

- An HDM family diet-planner (e.g., mother and father jointly) who may seriously revise their family's diet as a result of some government-appointed committee with recommendations for family diet-planners,
- Medical specialists who may or may not adopt a proposed new treatment for a deadly disease, and
- A financial decision support team that is concerned with how to model asset-class returns in a simulation model used to advise investors of the long-run consequences of one or another investment strategy.

As illustrated above, statistical results may go to an intermediary person or group that evaluates, or further processes, the results before they are passed on, to be used by or on behalf of the ultimate HDM client. The above examples included the government-appointed nutritional panel that evaluated the statistical results, perhaps along with competing or complementary analyses; the design committee that designed the financial decision support system that included the simulation model, such as the GuidedChoice DSS described in Chapter 7 (Volume II); and a medical board that decided how to advise specialists in the field, and then the individual specialist who made up his or her mind as to what to recommend to the patient in each individual case.

HDMs have priors, whether or not they know what a "prior" is. Some research results seem more plausible than others to a particular HDM, ranging from "Of course" to "I doubt that." This suggests that HDMs should be informed as to how compelling the evidence is for the results of a statistical analysis, e.g., what is the chance that if they had acted on the advice, they would be subsequently informed that the results were wrong.

HDM decisions depend in part on tastes and situation: For example, one family or individual may find a proposed shift in diet "no big deal," while for another it may represent a major lifestyle change. The urgency of adopting a proposed new cure may depend on a specific patient's condition (e.g., whether or not he or she is allergic to the standard alternative treatment).

The impact on portfolio risk-return of the decision to use a particular return generation model will usually depend on whether the model is used to select a highly leveraged or tightly constrained portfolio. Such matters of "taste and situation" are formalized in the RDM theory recounted in this book as the utilities the RDM attaches to various outcomes. Thus, we need to judge whether a particular statistical procedure will well suit HDMs with a variety of tastes and situations as well as a variety of views as to what are plausible hypotheses. In short, I will view the various statistical procedures from the Hildreth (1963) "remote Bayes'" clients point of view (POV) presented in Chapter 5 (in Volume I). While Chapter 5, following Markowitz and Usmen (1996a, 1996b) and Markowitz, Tessitore. Tessitore, and Usmen (2014), used particular procedures to serve remote Bayesians, the remote Bayesian POV is not a procedure but an objective. Perhaps HDMs approximating RDMs with differing utility functions and priors would be better served by using different—or perhaps just additional—statistical procedures. As already noted, this chapter will examine such procedures.

R. A. FISHER AND NEYMAN-PEARSON HYPOTHESIS TESTS

The Neyman-Pearson test procedure is considered by many (including me) to be an attractive refinement of the R. A. Fisher test of significance, although Fisher never saw it that way (Fisher 1960). Both procedures classify possible observations into two sets: an *accept* region and a *reject* region. The Neyman-Pearson forms attest regions so as to be efficient in terms of the two types of errors, whereas Fisher formed his test regions by different criteria. I will discuss serious problems with the Neyman-Pearson procedure, but the same arguments apply to Fisher's tests as well.

The Neyman-Pearson procedure can grossly mislead one as to how a Bayesian should shift beliefs given evidence. For example, suppose that there are two hypotheses, H_1 and H_2, and three possible observations, O_1, O_2, and O_3, with $P(O|H)$ given in Table 18.1a.

The set $\{O_1, O_2\}$ is a Neyman-Pearson test region for H_1 with size = 5%. It is the "most powerful" test of this size because it gathers together the observations (two in this case) with the lowest ratios of $P(O_i|H_1)$ to $P(O_i|H_2)$. In particular, if O_2 is observed, the test rejects H_1 at the 5% level. To some this might suggest that a Bayesian should shift belief by a factor of 19:1 against H_1 in favor of H_2. But $P(O_2|H_1)/P(O_2|H_2)$ beliefs should be shifted by a factor of four against H_2 *in favor* of H_1!

TABLE 18.1A

	H_1	H_2
O_1	.01	.98
O_2	.04	.01
O_3	.95	.01

The above example has the virtue of being simple and the drawback of not being "realistic," that is, not drawn from actual practice. Edwards, Lindman, and Savage (1963) examine tests used in practice and find that the Bayesian shift in odds ratio is typically much less than the classical p-value or size of the test and that it illustrates "how classically significant values of t can, in realistic cases, be based on data that actually favor the null hypothesis." Lindley (1957, p. 190) shows that there is no limit to how misleading an R. A. Fisher p-value or Neyman-Pearson test size can be. He considers a test of the hypothesis that unknown mean $\theta = \theta_0$ for a sample of size n drawn from a normal population with known variance σ^2. The Bayesian is assumed to attach a probability c to $\theta = \theta_0$ and to have a prior density $p(\theta)$ on a finite interval I that includes θ_0. Bounded $p(\theta)$ is sufficient but not necessary for the Lindley argument. Depending on n, the posterior belief $\bar{c}$ of the Bayesian proposition that $\theta = \theta_0$ may be arbitrarily close to 1. Lindley provides a numerical example, with $\sigma^2 = 1$, $c = \frac{1}{2}$ and the observation just significant at the 5% level of a two-sided test. "[F]or small samples (n ≤ 10) the probability of θ_0 has decreased appreciably from its initial value of ½. . . . For medium samples (10 < n < 100) the probability has only decreased a little. . . . By the time n has reached a value of 300, $\bar{c}$ is equal to c." For larger n, the classical statistician has rejected $\theta = \theta_0$ at the 5% level, whereas the Bayesian has increased the probability attached to that hypothesis.

The fact that the Bayesian view and the "objectivist" view come to different—in some cases, radically different—conclusions from the same data does not prove that one is right and the other is wrong. It merely shows that they are different. At least one—possibly—can give bad advice. In the following section, I present the standard Bayesian view of what is wrong with the objectivist approach. In the following section, I also present and respond to R. A. Fisher's argument against what he calls "inverse probability," i.e., inference based on Bayes's theorem.

THE LIKELIHOOD PRINCIPLE

A principal difference between the Bayesian calculation, on the one hand, and the Fisher and Neyman-Pearson inference, by contrast, is that the former uses only $P(O|H)$ for the observation that actually occurred, i.e., $P(O_2|H_1)$ and $P(O_2|H_2)$ in the example. The Fisher and Neyman-Pearson tests, on the other hand, depend in part on the probabilities of outcomes that did not occur. In other words, they violate what I define as the "likelihood principle," namely that any conclusion (and action) should depend on the ability of alternate hypotheses to explain the data observed.

As discussed in the preceding section, with $P(O_i|H_j)$ as specified in Table 18.1a, the Fisher and Neyman-Pearson tests would reject Hypothesis 1 if O_2 is observed. Compare this with the $P(O_i|H_j)$ in Table 18.1b. The probabilities of observing O_2 given H_1 or H_2—namely $P(O_1|H_2)$, $P(O_2|H_2)$ and $P(O_3|H_2)$—are the same as in Table 18.1a. All that has changed is that the probability distribution given H_1 has more weight in O_1—namely, now $P(O_1|H_1) = .05$ rather than .01—with the extra .04 probability having been "borrowed" from $P(O_3|H_1)$. Now O_1 by itself is the 5% critical region. Observation 2 is in the *accept* rather than *reject* region, even though the probabilities of getting O_2 given H_1 or H_2 have not changed.

TABLE 18.1B

	H_1	H_2
O_1	.05	.98
O_2	.04	.01
O_3	.91	.01

In Table 18.1c, part of the increase in $P(O_1|H_1)$, as compared to Table 18.1a, is "borrowed" from $P(O_2|H_1)$. Now the probability of O_2 is no greater given H_1 or H_2, yet the Neyman-Pearson tests accept H_1 for probabilities in Table 18.1c and reject it in the case of those in Table 18.1a.

TABLE 18.1C

	H_1	H_2
O_1	.05	.98
O_2	.01	.01
O_3	.94	.01

As already noted, for us the "likelihood principle" may be stated as follows: Rational choice (e.g., by the consumers of a given statistical analysis) should depend on the probabilities that various hypotheses have for "explaining" the observation actually observed, not on their abilities not observed. (Recall, the setup is such that one and only one observation occurs, and "nothing happened is a possible observation.")

Compare this with the usual account of the scientific method, as, e.g., Karl Popper (1963) would tell us. Specifically, consider the following three hypotheses concerning gravity, namely

H_1: Newton's action-at-a-distance hypothesis, which proposes that the gravitational force between two bodies is directly proportional to the product of their masses and inversely proportional to their distances

$$f : m_1 m_2 / d^2$$

H_2: Einstein's theory of curved space-time

H_3: Action at a distance, such as that postulated by Newton, but with force inversely proportional to the *cube* of the distance between the bodies

$$f : m_1 m_2 / d^3$$

Possible observations $O_1, O_2, \ldots, O_M$ (for some huge M) are the various measurements that *could* have been recorded concerning the movements of the planets about the sun *and* the deflection of light when passing near the sun. The actual observation, O^*, is the actually observed planetary motions and deflection of light. Hypothesis 2, Einstein's curved space-time hypothesis, is the currently accepted hypothesis based on the actual observation O^*. (Caveats: Newton's hypothesis is retained as a useful approximation for most day-to-day conditions, and Einstein's hypothesis may itself someday be overturned. But, for the present, O^* is the observation, and H_2 is the accepted hypothesis.)

Note that the issue of whether H_1, H_2, or H_3 could explain any observation that *did not occur* is not considered relevant to the acceptance of H_2 based on O^*. This is in contrast to "objective" statistical procedures that accept or reject H_2 in Tables 18.1a, b, and c when O_2 is observed depending on $P(O_1|H_1)$ and $P(O_3|H_1)$. I assume that the reader agrees that whether or not a family should alter their diet, a financial DSS design team should use a particular return-generation model, or a specialist should use a proposed medical procedure (assuming in each case that it is represented by accepting or rejecting H_1 in favor of H_2 in Tables 18.1a, b, and c) should not depend on shifts in the ability of H_1 and H_2 to explain O_1 and O_3, had they occurred a fortiori, as illustrated by Tables 18.1a versus 18.1b), and a decrease in the ability of H_1 to explain the actual observation should not be considered favorable to the H_1 hypothesis.

ANDREI KOLMOGOROV

The word "probability" is used throughout this four-volume book. For example, in Chapter 19 I discuss whether the concept of "objective" *probability* makes sense and why *weights* in a certain equation should be interpreted as *probabilities*. It is necessary, therefore, for me to define what I mean by probability. Note: I am not required here to survey how everybody else—or anybody else—uses the term. What I must do is tell you how I—me, Harry Markowitz, personally—use the term here and now. The answer is that the word "probability" will refer to its use in *any application*—whether the originally intended one or not—*in which I apply the first five axioms of the Kolmogorov* (1932) *six-axiom system.* I will refer to this five-axiom version of Kolmogorov (1932) as K32. As usual, the fact that the first five axioms are *required*, but the sixth is not required, does not preclude Kolmogorov's sixth axiom from also holding in specific applications.

The left column of Exhibit 18.1 presents the six axioms of K32, labeled I through VI, as in Kolmogorov (1933). These are divided here—as in Kolmogorov—between the first five, which apply to sample spaces generally—*whether the sample space is finite or not*—and Axiom VI, which imposes a requirement on probability measure in nonfinite sample spaces. (Axiom VI is satisfied trivially for finite sample spaces.) If we confine ourselves to finite sample spaces, then Kolmogorov's first five axioms are equivalent to the characterization presented in Chapter 8 (in Volume 2), wherein nonnegative probabilities, summing to 1.0, are assigned to each sample point, and the probability assigned to each subset of the sample space is the sum of the probabilities of the sample points contained in the subset. The right column of Exhibit 18.1 summarizes how the K32 axioms are a special-case for finite populations. Kolmogorov (1932) acknowledges the precedence of Henri Lebesgue (1902) and Maurice Fréchet (1904) in providing the technical apparatus used by Kolmogorov to show that his six simple axioms are sufficient to describe any probability application (e.g. many-dimensional, continuous-time stochastic processes) no matter how complex.

The reason I exclude Kolmogorov's Axiom VI from K32, rather than just ignore it because I usually restrict discussions

EXHIBIT 18.1 Kolmogorov Axioms and Their Finite Special Case

Kolmogorov Axioms	Finite Special Case
Let E be a collection of elements . . . which we shall call elementary events and F a set of subsets of E; the elements of the set F will be called random events E.	E is a set of elementary, indivisible "sample points." E is called the "sample space." F is the set of all subsets E.
I. F is a field of independent sets.	1. As noted already, F is the set of all subsets of E.
II. F contains the set E.	2. Corollary of Axiom I.
III. To each set A in F is assigned a nonnegative real number P(A). This number P(A) is called the "probability" of the event A.	3. Applies *as* is to the finite case.
IV. P(E) equals 1.	4. Same as 3.
V. If A and B have no element in common, then $P(A + B) = P(A) + P(B)$.	5. Same as 3.
VI. For a decreasing sequence of events $A_1 \supset A_2 \supset \ldots \supset A_n \ldots$ of F, for which $\cap A_n = 0$, the following equation holds: $\lim P(A_n) = 0, n \to \infty$.	6. Trivially satisfied in finite sample spaces.

to finite sample spaces, is because there are two kinds of probability applications involved: one commonly used in practice, the other proposed as an alternative, on philosophical
grounds. The distinction between the two involves the concept of a *countable* set. Recall from the previous chapter that a
countable set (of any type of object) is one that can be placed
in one-to-one correspondence with the "natural numbers,"
i.e., the positive integers. In particular, the rational numbers
are countable, and the irrational numbers are not. A probability measure is "finitely additive" if, for any *finite* collection S_1,
$S_2, \ldots, S_n$ in F (in Exhibit 18.1) such that

$$S_i \cap S_j = 0 \qquad \text{for } i \neq j \tag{18.1a}$$

i.e., no two sets have a point in common, we have:

$$\text{Prob}\left(\bigcup_{i=1}^{n} S_i\right) = \sum_{i=1}^{n} \text{Prob}(S_i) \tag{18.1b}$$

A probability measure is *countably* additive if, in addition
to (Equation 18.1b), for any *countable* sequence of sets $S1, S2, \ldots$,
$\in$ F such that condition (Equation 18.1a) holds, we have

$$\text{Prob}\left(\bigcup_{i=1}^{n} S_i\right) = \sum_{i=1}^{\infty} \text{Prob}(S_i) \tag{18.1c}$$

Countably additive measures are finitely additive, but
not vice versa. The probability distributions one usually meets

in statistics or stochastic processes are countably additive, but some notable axiom systems imply only finitely additive probability measures. In particular, see the Savage (1954) discussion of finite additivity. I omit the Kolmogorov Axiom VI from what I here call K32 so as not to have my definition of probability exclude finitely additive measures.

Kolmogorov's objective in presenting these axioms was to establish a solid, logical foundation for probability theory, comparable to Hilbert's foundations for geometry. Specifically, Kolmogorov's Preface tells us:

> *The purpose of this monograph is to give an axiomatic foundation for the theory of probability. The author set himself the task of putting in their natural place, among the general notions of modern mathematics, the basic concepts of probability theory—concepts which until recently were considered to be quite peculiar.*
>
> *This task would have been a rather hopeless one before the introduction of Lebesgue's theories of measure and integration. However, after Lebesgue's publication of his investigations, the analogies between measure of a set and probability of an event, and between integral of a function and mathematical expectation of a random variable, became apparent. These analogies allowed of further extensions: thus, for example, various properties of independent random variables were seen to be in complete analogy*

with the corresponding properties of orthogonal functions. But if probability theory was to be based on the above analogies, it still was necessary to make the theories of measure and integration independent of the geometric elements which were in the foreground with Lebesgue. This has been done by Fréchet.

On page 1 of the text itself, Kolmogorov tells us:

The theory of probability, as a mathematical discipline, can and should be developed from axioms in exactly the same way as Geometry and Algebra. This means that after we have defined the elements to be studied and their basic relations, and have stated the axioms by which these relations are to be governed, all further exposition must be based exclusively on these axioms, independent of the usual concrete meaning of these elements and their relations.

In accordance with the above, in §1 the concept of a field of probabilities is defined as a system of sets which satisfies certain conditions. What the elements of this set represent is of no importance in the purely mathematical development of the theory of probability (cf. the introduction of basic geometric concepts in the The Foundation of Geometry by Hilbert, or the definitions of groups, rings and fields in abstract algebra).

Every axiomatic (abstract) theory admits, as is well known, of an unlimited number of concrete interpretations besides those from which it was derived. Thus we find applications in fields of science which have no relation to the concepts of random event and of probability in the precise meaning of these words.

A MODEL OF MODELS

An entity M is a model *of* some phenomena P if there are "variables" in M that are identified as corresponding to variables in P. A "model" is any entity M that *potentially could be* a model **of** some phenomenon P. Clearly the prior two sentences need to be parsed.

1. A "model" M, or "phenomenon," is a system that contains entities of various types, connected by one-one, one-many, many-one, and many-many relationships.

2. Recall that EAS-E attributes are either many-one or one-one relationships, that EAS-E sets are one-many relationships, and that I show in an endnote how any many-many relationships can always be viewed as two viewed one-many relationships.

3. An "application area" (AA) is defined by specifying what phenomenon, P (i.e., what "observations"), is within the provenance of the AA. (In practice, this specification is subject to various caveats. I will ignore these caveats in the formal theory of "what is

a model," lest I have to produce a "theory of caveats," which of course would have its own caveats.

4. If M is a model of the phenomena, P, in some AA, then there must be some implications of M observable in the P of the AA. That is, there must be one or more relationships (1–1, 1–n, n–1, or m—n) between entities and their relations in M and sequences of observations in P.

Newton's World, for Example

In Newton's world, the World System has a real-valued attribute called "Time." This system owns two sets, namely a set of points and a set of particles. The sets in the SIMSCRIPT programming languages contain a finite number of members (including zero as a finite number). Otherwise, the execution of a FOR EACH OF SET phrase would take forever. On the other hand, models of space can, and do, contain an infinite number of the entity type, POINT. Thanks to Descartes, individual points are characterized by three numbers

$$P = (X_1, X_2, X_3)$$

(a.k.a. x, y, z). This Cartesian characterization of points in space introduces another type of entity, namely the coordinate system. While the concept of a coordinate system has played a critical role in the development of mathematical applications in general, and physics in particular, it is not essential to the description of space. Euclid got along perfectly well without it.

However, I cannot spell out in detail here the minimum number of Euclidean concepts used in Newton's model. Specifically, every (point, Point) pair has an attribute, Distance. In order to characterize the EAS properties of Euclidean distance, I would have to introduce certain others and their EAS properties, namely Line, Angle, Triangle, Right-Angled Triangle, and, finally, arguably the most important mathematical discovery of all time, the Pythagorean Theorem. It would seem that I could bypass this whole mess by accepting the Cartesian characterization of space and arbitrarily defining distance as did Descartes. This could be justified by invoking Hilbert's principle, that a model is an arbitrary creation, as distinguished from a hypothesis that assigns a model to some phenomenon, identifying particular quantities in the model to observable quantities in the phenomenon.

But that would not do. In the next section I speak of the intended general application of a model—its IGA. For example, the words "point," "line," "triangle," and "distance" were used by Euclid without distinguishing between the model in the abstract and his particular application of this model. We now make that distinction. But the words "Point," "Line," etc. reflect the model's IGA. Its IGA also includes the words, concepts, and relationships Length, Angle, Axioms, Definitions, Theorem, Postulates, Proof, and **QED**. In particular, one needs the definitions of Axioms, Theorems, Definitions (within the Euclidian system), and Right Triangle for the statement and

Euclidean proof of the Pythagorean hypothesis. Without spelling out the details, then, I assume that the IGA is Euclid's three-dimensional geometry.

Sometimes something that is not assumed is as important as things that are assumed. This is because the IGAs of other models make the assumption, and it is important that the model in question and its IGA do not.

THE R.A. FISHER ARGUMENT

The fact that the objectivist view of inference is seriously flawed does not prove that the subjectivist view is not equally flawed. As in a political debate, I need not only present the virtues of my candidate but also rebut (or concede) any vices claimed by my candidate's opponents or doubters. In Chapter 17, I argued the virtues of Bayesian inference by presenting four axioms concerning the relationship between opportunity and action that any RDM would want to satisfy and then showed that any such relationship between opportunity and action must be "Bayesian." I also noted the Ellsberg objection to our Axiom 2 and argued that while HDMs may violate this axiom, RDMs would not.

In addition to being generally recognized as a proponent of objectivism as a movement, Fisher was a vocal critic of Bayesian inference, which he refers to as "inverse probability." In particular, in his 1930 article, "Inverse Probability," he lays out his case against the use of Bayes's law for inference and in favor of what he calls "fiducial probability." In a section titled,

"The Rejection of Inverse Probability," on page 6 of Fisher (1960), he presents a brief summary of his ongoing position on the subject. In particular, he says:

> *The discrepancy of opinion among historical writers on probability is so great that to mention the subject is unavoidable. It would, however, be out of place here to argue the point in detail. I will only state three considerations which will explain why, in the practical applications of the subject I shall not assume the truth of Bayes's axiom. Two of these reasons would, I think, be generally admitted, but the first, I can well imagine, might be indignantly repudiated in some quarters.*

In this section, I will review Fisher's major argument, found in Fisher (1930) and then consider each of the arguments in the latter.

In Fisher (1930), he primarily considers the case of alternative probability distributions involving (e.g.) a continuous random variable with a density function f(x) that depends on parameters θ_1, θ_2, . . . that themselves have a continuous range. He notes that Bayes's law would apply if these parameters were drawn randomly from a super-population of density

$$dF = \Psi(\theta_1, \theta_2, \theta_3, \dots)$$

Fisher then says that the argument in support of inverse probability says

something equivalent to "We do not know the function
Ψ specifying the super-population, but in view of our
ignorance of the actual values of θ we may take Ψ to
be constant." Perhaps we might add that all values of θ
being equally possible their probabilities are by defini-
tion equal; but however we might disguise it, the choice
of this particular a priori distribution for the θ's is just
as arbitrary as any other could be. If we were, for exam-
ple, to replace our θ's by an equal number of functions
of them, θ$_1$, θ$_2$, θ$_3$, . . . all objective statements could be
translated from the one notation to the other, but the
simple assumption Ψ(θ$_1$, θ$_2$, θ$_3$, . . .) = constant may
translate into a most complicated frequency function
for

$$\theta_1, \theta_2, \theta_3.$$

Or, to put it another way, a given set of distributions can always be parameterized in more than one way: The posterior distribution one gets from a given likelihood function may be radically different depending on whether, e.g., θ$_1$, θ$_2$, . . . has a uniform prior or whether θ$_1$, θ$_2$, . . . does. This is a serious concern that will be discussed at length in the next section.

After the above-quoted passage, Fisher continues:

The first is this: The axiom leads to apparent math-
ematical contradictions. In explaining these contra-
dictions away, advocates of inverse probability seem

forced to regard mathematical probability, not as an objective quantity measured by observable frequencies, but as measuring merely psychological tendencies, theorems respecting which are useless for scientific purposes.

I do not know what Fisher refers to when he speaks of "Bayes's axiom." In particular, the famous Bayes (1763) article, published posthumously, makes no mention of "An Axiom." Lest I missed something in my own reading of the Bayes article, I am delighted to defer to Edwards, Lindman, and Savage (1963), who note that, in fact,

Bayes's theorem is a simple and fundamental fact about probability that seems to have been clear to Thomas Bayes when he wrote his famous article published in 1763 (recently reprinted), though he did not state it there explicitly.

I assume that Bayes's axiom here is the assumption that all hypotheses are equal, as Pierre-Simon Laplace (see MacTutor 1999) assumed. The contradiction that follows from this assumption is that if the parameter space is unbounded, then it cannot be true that all hypotheses are equally likely; e.g., if the parameter space S consists of the real line R, or the nonnegative "half" of the real line, it cannot be true that one's prior distribution is uniform, since if the identity function f is positive; i.e., if

$$f(x) > 0 \qquad \text{for all } x \in S$$
$$\text{Prob } (x \in S) = \infty$$

whereas if

$$f(x) = 0 \qquad \text{for all } x \in S$$

then

$$\text{Prob } (x \in S) = 0$$

The obvious way out of this dilemma is to not assume that an RDM's prior is uniformly distributed over the entire parameter space but rather that it is locally uniformly distributed; i.e., it is uniform in a large bounded interval that includes all values of x with nonnegligible $P(O|x)$ and is irrelevant beyond this interval. As Edwards, Lindman, and Savage (1963) puts it

> *To ignore the departures from uniformity, it suffices that your actual prior density change gently in the region favored by the data and not itself too strongly favor some other region.*

In other words—given certain broad conditions, that Edwards, Lindman, and Savage (1963) state verbally here and spell out mathematically in their section title, "The Principle of Stable Estimation" (page 202)—one may assume that priors are *locally* uniform. The *local uniformity* "parry" to the "thrust" that a prior distribution cannot be globally uniform seems so obvious that it is hard to believe that no one "who indignantly repudiated" Fisher's position came up with it.

The Savage axioms (and ours) imply that an RDM should act according to a EU/PB maximum, where PB included (or consists entirely of, in Savage's view) what Savage refers to as "personal probabilities." Fisher says that "theorems respecting which are useless for scientific purposes." Of Fisher's three reasons for rejecting inverse probability, this is the most serious charge: that all conclusions produced by statistical analysis that admit of personal probability must necessarily reflect the analyst's personal opinions. To a certain extent this has to be true for any statistical analysis, that analysts' views are reflected in the choices of the topic, the data set, and the hypotheses to be tested. But allowing for this—i.e., for a given topic, data, and set of hypotheses, the Bayes factors summarized for remote clients by the specific "remote client approach" are *objective* statistical quantities. All clients add their own priors.

In comparing two simple hypotheses, no assumption need be made as to the remote client's priors. For example, Markowitz and Usmen (1996a, 1996b) report that the Bayes facts between the two hypotheses

H_1, the LH maximizing normal distribution, and

H_2, a Student-t distribution with 4.5 degrees of freedom

are about 10^{72}. Thus an RDM would shift the odds ratio that it attaches to $P(H_1/P(1 + 2)$ by this factor. On the other hand,

Markowitz and Usmen (1996a, 1996b) invoke the principle of stable estimation in reporting the Bayes factor between two compound hypotheses; and would have also invoked it in computing the Bayes factor between a simple hypothesis and a compound hypothesis.

There is some flexibility in *how* to apply the locally uniform assumption. For example, for Student-t distributions with finite skewness measure

$$M_4 = \frac{E(r-E)^2}{\alpha^2}$$

Table 5.3 in Chapter 5 of Volume I (page 167), shows the likelihood of the Markowitz and Usmen S_1 sample for the Student-t distribution for both various degrees of freedom, df, and the corresponding M_4. We see that $M_4 \rightarrow \infty$ as df $\rightarrow$ 4. For df $\leq$ 4, M_4 cannot be used as a parameter, since it is undefined. But to illustrate the effect of nonlinear relationships between two different ways of parameterizing a family of distributions, suppose that two Bayesian statisticians agree that M_4 lies in the interval (7, 1,000); one assumes that—within this interval and its corresponding df interval—the prior is uniformly distributed as a function of M4; whereas the other assumes that it is uniformly distributed as a function of σ. The integral

$$\int f(x)LH(x)dx$$

will be much smaller under the uniform M_4 than under the uniform σ, since the former assigns a greater prior weight to a region of smaller posterior probability.

Fisher continues:

> *My second reason is that it is the nature of an axiom that its truth should be apparent to any rational mind that fully apprehends its meaning. The axiom of Bayes has certainly been fully apprehended by a good many rational minds, including that of its author, without carrying this conviction of necessary truth. This, alone, shows that I cannot be accepted as the axiomatic basis of a rigorous argument.*

The approach adopted in this volume is *not* to take Bayes's rule (with or without the assumption of equal priors) as axiomatic but to deduce from axioms that (for some version of which) many find plausible. Some (such as Maurice Allais [1953]) don't: But you can't win them all when it comes to value judgments.

Finally, Fisher notes:

> *My third reason is that inverse probability has been only very rarely used in the justification of conclusions from experimental facts, although the theory has been widely taught, and is widespread in the literature of probability. Whatever the reasons are which give experimenters confidence that they can draw valid conclusions from their results, they seem*

to act just as powerfully whether the experimenter
has heard of the theory of inverse probability or not.

This begs the question as to whether Fisher's followers have been following a true or false prophet.

Let us return to the point that both Fisher's objective procedures and the remote Bayes procedures advocated in this volume report objective probabilities, which is a better guide to HDM action.

BAYESIAN CONJUGATE PRIOR PROCEDURES

The Markowitz and Usmen companion article (1996a, 1996b) which followed was concerned with advising readers as to which models of stock market return distributions to use and how to weight their results in applications such as the choice of strategy for buying and selling options on the S&P 500 Index. These readers are "remote clients" in the sense of Hildreth (1963). We do not know their priors, which presumably vary from one to another. Since they are only pale imitations of RDMs, they typically have only vague ideas of their own priors.

We will not tell the remote clients what their posterior beliefs should be, given our data. Rather, we will advise on shifts in beliefs. According to Bayes's rule, if H_1 and H_2 are two hypotheses, given a sample S, their posterior odds ratio $P(H_1|S)/P(H_2|S)$ is related to their *a priori* odds $P(H_1)/P(H_2)$ by

$$\frac{P(H_1|S)}{P(H_2|S)} = \frac{P(S|H_1)}{P(S|H_2)} \Psi \frac{P(H_1)}{P(H_2)}$$

$P(S|H_1)/P(S|H_2)$ is known as the "Bayes factor." We shall also refer to it as the "shift in belief Ψ (H_1, H_2) from H_2 to H_1."

When H_1 and H_2 are simple hypotheses, Ψ does not depend on priors. For example, confining ourselves for the present to t with $\Delta_T = 1$ (weekdays), let $H_1 = \{y,$ is i.i.d. normal with mean $\mu = 5.45$ (10^{-4}) and standard deviation $\sigma = 7.68$ $(10^{-3})\}$.

$H_2 = \{y,$ is i.i.d. Student-t with mean and variance as in H_1 and $M_4 = 12\}$, where M_4 is the normalized fourth moment $E(y - \mu1)^4/\sigma^4$, a.k.a. β_2 or $\gamma_2 + 3$. Then, for a sample to be described in the companion article, Ψ (H_1, H_2) $= 10^{-74}$. If an RDM had considered H_1 10^9 to be more probable prior to the sample, she or he would think H_2 10^{65} to be more probable thereafter.

If $H_3 = \{$i.i.d. Pearson Type IV with mean, variance and M_4 as in H_2 and $M_3 = 0.038\}$, where M_3, the normalized third moment is $E(y - \mu_1)^3/\sigma^3$ (a.k.a. $\gamma_1 = \sqrt{\beta_2}$), then Ψ (H_3, H_2) $= 1.06$. An RDM would shift the odds ratio by a factor of 1.06 in favor of the slightly skewed Type IV distribution against the symmetric Student-t.

Throughout we shall speak of shifts of belief rather than accepting or rejecting a hypothesis. In general, even if the odds ratio between any two hypotheses H and K should be shifted by a factor of Ψ(H, K) $= .95/.05 = 19$ (as the classical rejection of K at the 5% level *sounds* as if it implies), K should not necessarily be treated as if it had a posterior probability of zero. Suppose that H was a normal distribution and K a long-tailed distribution such as H_2 or H_3. Suppose that the prior odds ratio was 1:1, and therefore, the posterior odds 19:1. For some strategies with options and futures, a many-a move in the Index can be disastrous, while, for other strategies, a many-a move is beneficial or benign. Consequently, expected utilities of different strategies may rank quite differently for posterior probabilities $(p_H, P_K) = (1, 0)$ than for $(.95, .05)$.

The problem is not alleviated by choosing a different significance level. It might seem that if a shift of 19:1 is not sufficient to reject, i.e., henceforth to ignore, the unfavored hypothesis; then perhaps a larger shift, say 99:1, should be used. But the statement that K has been rejected at the 1% level—now defined as $\Psi(H, K) \geq 99$—does not tell us whether $\Psi = 101$ or 10^{70}, and nonrejection doesn't tell us whether $\Psi = 98$ or 1.06 or 10^{70}. Assuming a prior of 1:1 to be specific, a posterior odds ratio of 10^{70}:1 may have different practical consequences than 101:1 and an odds ratio of 10^{-70}:1 different practical consequences than 98:1. Finally, it will typically make little practical difference whether the posterior odds ratio is 101:1 or 98:1, though the former would reject and the latter accept at the 1% level. Thus, the information that a hypothesis has been rejected or not at some preassigned level is usually much less informative than the value of Ψ, or even the order of magnitude of Ψ.

For compound hypotheses H and K, Ψ depends on priors within $H \cup K$ but not outside it. Specifically,

$$\Psi(H, K) = \frac{\int_H P(S|\theta)dP(\theta)}{\int_K P(S|\theta)d(P\theta)}$$

where H and K may be subsets of the same or different parameter spaces. Suppose, for example, that

$$H = \{y \text{ is i.i.d. normal}\}$$
$$K = \{y \text{ is i.i.d. Pearson with } M_4 = 12\}$$

The shift $\Psi(H, K)$ depends on the prior distribution $\tilde{p}(M_3)$ $= p(\mu_0, \sigma_0, M_3, 12)$ for any given μ_0, σ_0. A frequent practice is to assume, with Jeffreys (1939), that priors are diffuse, e.g.,

$$\tilde{p}(M_3) = 1$$

This is an improper prior in that $\int \tilde{p}(M_3)dM_3 = \infty$. Improper priors can lead to strange results (see, e.g., Buehler 1959, and Lindley 1972). To avoid such strange results, it is sometimes argued that the implications for action of an improper prior should be considered as the limit of the implications for action of increasingly diffuse but proper priors such as

$$\tilde{p}(M_3) = 1/(m_{H1}, m_{LOW}) \text{ on } [m_{LOW}, m_{H1}]$$

as $m_{H1} \to \infty$, $m_{LOW} \to \infty$.

Even though for a wide range of plausible M_3 likelihoods $P(S|\mu_0, M_3, 12) >> P(S|\mu_0, \sigma_0,), 3)$, prior (3) as discussed and enumerated in Markowitz Usmen (1996a and 1996b) implies $\Psi(H, K) = \infty$. The posterior odds are 1:0 in favor of the normal. For priors of the form (4) also as discussed and enumerated in Markowitz Usmen (1996a and 1996b), $\Psi \to \infty$ as either $m_{LOW} \to -\infty$ or $m_{H1} \to \infty$ or both. On the other hand, we conjecture that most readers have priors which assign a nonnegligible, positive probability to some moderately sized interval $M_3 \in [\underline{m}, \overline{m}]$. Specifically, we propose in the companion article, (Markowitz and Usmen 1996a, 1996b) that the reader has a prior probability of *at least* .01 for the interval $(-2.667, 2.667]$. To visualize this interval, note that -2.667 and 2.667 are the M_3 values for binomial distributions with $p = .1$ and $.9$, respectively. Based on this assumption, and other assumptions which favor the normal distribution, i.e., will not overstate the shift against the normal, we compute that the shift for K against the normal hypothesis H is at least 10^{69}. Thus, for readers who find the proposed inequality acceptable, (3) and (4)—again, see Markowitz Usmen (1996a and 1996b)—imply the wrong conclusion concerning $\Psi, (H, K)$.

An approach frequently recommended for Bayesian inference is to use a conjugate prior (see DeGroot 1970, Zellner 1971, Berger 1985). But no nontrivial conjugate prior is available for the entire Pearson family. Another approach is to compute worst (or best) case shifts; i.e., to determine the prior which maximizes the shift for H against K or for K against H (Berger and Sellke 1987). This is highly commendable if the best-case and worst-case Ψ are close, but in our example the best case for H is the diffuse prior with $\Psi(H, K) = \infty$, whereas the best case for K concentrates M_3 near .04 and has $\Psi(H, K)$ of about 10^{74}.

Still another approach, "stable estimation," recommended by Edwards, Lindman, and Savage (1963), plays an important role in Markowitz Usmen (1996a and 1996b) with respect to both simple and compound hypotheses. In particular, we note in Markowitz Usmen (1996a and 1996b) that if the principle of stable estimation applies to H and, separately, to K as well, then Ψ takes on a relatively simple form even when H and K are of high dimension. This is of general methodical interest, but it is convenient to postpone its discussion until the Markowitz and Usmen article's section on shifts of belief between compound hypotheses.

Edwards, Lindman, and Savage (1963) define the "principle of stable estimation" in terms of conditions under which the posterior distribution is approximately proportional to the likelihood function: that is, to a reasonable approximation, the prior distribution may be assumed uniform over some finite range beyond which LH is so small that $\int LH(\theta)p(\theta)d\theta$ may be assumed negligible. Briefly: "To ignore the departures from uniformity, it suffices that your actual prior density change gently in the region favored by the data and not itself too strongly favor some other region." Edwards, Lindman, and Savage (1963) then spell this out more formally. In the present case, we recommend the principle of stable estimation for approximating $p(\theta|S)$ as a function of μ, σ, M_3 *for any fixed* M_4, at least for subsamples S_1 and S_3.

19

EUDAIMONIA

REVIEW

In Chapter 13, we noted David Hume's (1962, 1739) distinction between two types of propositions:

- Relationships between ideas, as dealt with in logic and mathematics, and
- Assertions about matters of fact.

On the latter type of proposition, we noted as an example that, though we released the ball a thousand times—and though it fell toward the earth each of those times—that did not constitute a formal *proof* that, if released again, it would go down a thousand and first time.

There is a third type of proposition, namely that which asserts that you should

- Honor your father and mother,
- Not murder,

- Not commit adultery,
- Not steal,
- Not bear false witness, and
- Not covet your neighbor's wife.

These are moral commandments rather than assertions about matters of fact. I omit from the list of commandments such as you shall have no other gods before you, since this includes the assertion that gods (including *this* God) exist. Note that the first commandment does not assert that It is the *only* god, but only that "you" (we) should have no other god before It (Jehovah). Explicit monotheism came later. Other commandments included: You shall

- Make no idols,
- Not take the name of the lord in vain, and
- Keep holy the Sabbath day.

These implicitly assume that Jehovah exists, so they include a hypothesis about the existence of a deity as well as a moral injunction.

Later rules include Christ's injunction to "do unto others as you would have them do unto you." This moral rule is not to be taken literally. For example, a child is not enjoined to do unto his or her parents as its parents would do unto it. The child cannot go out and earn a living or manage a household, as its parents do or arrange to have done. Rather, the child should do unto the parent as it would have its child do unto it were it a parent. Such a more spelled-out prescription for moral behavior is most famously found in the teachings of Confucius (2014), who advised, for example, that a subject should not wear fancier clothes than the emperor.

Primitive tribes had rules. These rules typically distinguished between "us" and "them." For example, the reason why Moses did not live to see the "promised land" was that he failed to engage in a "holy war" against the Canaanites. There is clearly a sharp difference between the first four commandments that require the adherent to have no other gods before Him, make no idols, not take His name in vain, and keep the Sabbath, as compared to the injunctions to

- Honor thy father and mother,
- Not commit adultery,
- Not steal,
- Not bear false witness, and
- Not covet.

All human societies have rules. For example, all societies forbid incest. I have no idea what reasons primitive peoples gave for this prohibition, but we now know that inbreeding will perpetuate an undesirable trait that would likely be deleted from the population by natural selection.

Kant's (1943, 1781) "categorical imperative" directs us to each act in such a way that if all of us act that way it will benefit all of us. It is hard to distinguish that from "Do unto others as you would have others do unto you" suitably qualified in the manner of Aristotle or Confucius. E.g., if you are a professor, do unto your students as your favorite professors did unto you.[1]

EUDAIMONIA FOR THE MASSES

According to Adam Smith,

> Both Plato and Aristotle were deeply suspicious of the ability of the forces of material self-interest to generate a just and harmonious social order. Self-interest and the pursuit of financial gain, they thought, tended to go hand-in-hand, and the negative consequences of this were observable all around them.
>
> . . .
>
> To rein in self-interest and avoid the potential problems that its unrestrained exercise could cause, Plato and Aristotle advocated policies including a prohibition on lending at interest, the elimination of profits, and statutory fixing of prices—all of which they believed would help to keep commercial activity in check.
>
> . . .
>
> Given that politics and economics were part of the same body of analysis for Plato, it is not surprising that his distrust of self-interested individual action bled over into the political arena. The ideal state could not, for Plato, evolve via democratic

action; he opposed participatory governance and did
not believe that the citizens could understand how to
achieve the efficient outcomes of the ideal state unless
they submitted themselves to the guidance of a ruler
possessing superior intelligence.

Today, most of us would agree with a view that has been expressed by many, but most famously by Lord Acton, who essentially said, "Power corrupts. Absolute power corrupts absolutely." Judged by the number of people who seek to enter the United States, versus the number who seek to leave it, still, now, centuries after its founding, the United States is the embodiment of a successful political/economic theory, as expounded in the *Federalist Papers*, written by Alexander Hamilton, James Madison and John Jay (2014, 1788) and Adam Smith (2003, 1776). The "trick" is that a well-ordered market economy requires laws—equally applicable to all— that, on the one hand, make effective one's right to life, liberty and property and, on the other hand, constrain the economic (as well as other) actions of "the one" for the good of "the many." E.g., if using child labor, advertising cigarettes, selling narcotics, and not stopping at stop signs are democratically determined to be undesirable for "all," then they are forbidden to "all."

NOTES

Chapter 13

1. In this area, the generally accepted view is Hilbert's "modernized" version of the axiomatic method used by Euclid. I noted earlier in the preceding chapter that modern logic-systems fault Euclid for trying to *define* terms like "point" and "line" in terms that, themselves, are undefined. In contrast, Hilbert's geometry takes "point" and "line" as undefined terms and assumes certain axioms such as

    I.1. For every distinct two points A, B there exists a line that contains each of the points A, B.

    I.2 For every two distinct points A, B there exists no more than one line that contains each of the points A, B.

    Etc.

2. If, for example, a database contains 20 years of return data, but only for firms that existed 20 years before and are still in existence, and this database is used to test alternative policies, highly risky policies benefit, since the securities they select are guaranteed to be still in existence at the end of the data period.

Chapter 14

1. As an example of the mathematics that Bolzano was working on while he was professor of the philosophy of religion, here is a description of what he recorded in his notebook *Miscellanea Mathematica* in 1816. The description is by Joseph Dauben reviewing this material when it was first published in 1996:

> *Bolzano opens this notebook of Miscellanea Mathematica with notes on irrational and transcendental numbers and functions. But he was reading and recording his ideas on a host of other subjects as well, including the problem of how best to approach the proper mathematical understanding of zero; [Adrien-Marie] Legendre's work on surfaces, convexity, concavity, and conditions for congruity; analysis of other geometric concepts, including lengths, areas, volumes, and spheres; trigonometric formulas and spherical trigonometry; imaginary and exponential numbers; definition of the differential and discussion of the infinite and various opinions about it, as well as aspects of maxima and minima . . . Other topics covered here include various approaches to the calculus (including the method of exhaustion), and grounds for asserting the certainty of mathematics.*

> Axiom I *Axiom of extensionality.* If every element is a set M and is also an element of N and vice

versa, if, therefore, both $M \subset N$ and $N \subset M$, then always $M = N$; or, more briefly: Every set is determined by its elements.

Axiom II   *Axiom of elementary sets.* There exists a (fictitious) set, the null set, ø, that contains no element at all. If α is any object of the domain, there exists a set $\{\alpha\}$ containing α and only α as element; if a and b are any two objects of the domain, there always exists a set $\{a, b\}$ containing as elements a and b but no object x distinct from both.

Axiom III   *Axiom of separation.* Whenever the propositional function $F(x)$ is definite for all elements of a set M, M possesses a subset M_ς containing as elements precisely those elements x of M for which $F(x)$ is true.

Axiom IV   *Axiom of the power set.* To every set T there corresponds another set UT, the power set of T, that contains as elements precisely all subsets of T.

Axiom V   *Axiom of the union.* To every set T there corresponds a set T, the union of δT, that contains as elements precisely all elements of the elements of T.

Axiom VI   *Axiom of choice.* If T is a set whose elements all are sets that are different from 0 and mutually disjoint, its union δT includes at least one subset S_1 having one and only one element in common with each element of T.

Axiom VII   *Axiom of infinity.* There exists in the domain at least one set Z that contains the null set as an element and is so constituted that to each of its elements a there corresponds to a further element of the form {a}; in other words, that with each of its elements a it also contains the corresponding set {a} as an element.

Chapter 17

1. Markowitz (1959) made the more general assumption that the RDM could rank a convex *subset* of D. This "subset" could be D itself—i.e., other subsets were permitted as the set of alternatives among which the RDM had preferences—but D itself was not excluded. Therefore, any theorem proved in Markowitz (1959), Chapter 12, is also true of the more restrictive model postulated here. For convenience, the text calls the model presented here "M59" and discusses it as if it were the model present in Markowitz (1959), Chapter 12.

2.
$$
\begin{aligned}
\mathrm{Cov}(R_1, R_2) &= E[R_1 - E(R_1)][R_2 - E(R_2)] \\
&= E[R_1 - \mu_1 + \mu_1 - E(R_1)] \cdot [R_2 - \mu_2 + \mu_2 - E(R_2)] \\
&= E(R_1 - \mu_1)(R_2 - \mu_2) + E[\mu_1 - E(R_1)][\mu_2 - E(R_2)] \\
&\quad + E[R_1 - E(R_1)][\mu_2 - E(R_2)] \\
&\quad + E[R_2 - E(R_2)][\mu_1 - E(R_1)] \qquad (17.N1)
\end{aligned}
$$

The last two terms are zero; therefore,

$$Cov(R_1, R_2) = E\sigma_{ij} + Cov(\mu_i, \mu_j) \qquad (17.N2)$$

The first term on the right is the (subjective) average of "objective" covariances, whereas the second is the (subjective) covariance between the errors in the estimates of μ_i and μ_j. For example, the estimates of the expected returns for certain securities may come from a particular source or be produced by a particular methodology. The RDM may entertain the hypothesis that sometimes these estimates might be too high and sometimes too low, more than would be expected by chance. This would be reflected in the RDM's $Cov(\mu_i, \mu_j)$ belief, for R_i and R_j in this group.

3. Theorem:

$$If\{P\} = \{Q\}$$
$$and \{Q\} = \{R\}$$
$$then \{P\} = \{R\}$$

PROOF

I will show that Axioms I and II imply that if $\{P\} = \{Q\}$, then

$$\{pP + (1 - p)Q\} = \{P\}$$

The theorem is a corollary. Suppose, to the contrary, that

$$\{pP + (1 - p)Q\} > \{P\} = \{Q\}$$

Then, by Axiom II,

$$\{pP + (1 - p)\,Q\} > \{(1/2)[pP + (1 - p)Q]$$
$$+ (\tfrac{1}{2})Q\} > \{Q\} = \{P\}$$

But

$$(\tfrac{1}{2})[pP + (1 - p)Q] + (\tfrac{1}{2})Q = [(\tfrac{1}{2})p]P + [1 - (\tfrac{1}{2})p]Q$$

Hence

$$\{[(\tfrac{1}{2})p]P + [1 - (\tfrac{1}{2})p]Q\} > \{P\}$$

which implies, again by Axiom II, that

$$\left\{(\tfrac{1}{2}p)P + \left(1 - \tfrac{1}{2}p\right)Q\right\} > \frac{1 - p}{1 - (\tfrac{1}{2})p}\left[(\tfrac{1}{2}p)P + \right.$$
$$\left. (1 - \tfrac{1}{2}p)Q\right] + \left\{1 - \left[\frac{1 - p}{1 - (\tfrac{1}{2})p}\right]\right\}P$$

The expression on the right, however, is simply

$$pP + (1 - p)\,Q$$

Thus, we have

$$pP + (1 - p)Q > [(\tfrac{1}{2})p]P + [1 - (\tfrac{1}{2})p]Q > pP + (1 - p)Q$$

A contradiction.

Since the result would also have held if we had labeled it as Q, the distribution we had formerly called P, and vice versa, we may also conclude that

$$pP + (1 - p)\, Q] < P$$

Chapter 19

I find that the following principles help make for a mutually satisfactory teaching experience for you and your students.

First, and foremost, understand your topic thoroughly.

Second, prepare or carefully review, your lesson plans the night before. I learned this lesson the first time I taught a night course when I worked at the RAND Corporation in Santa Monica. I prepared my first lesson and it went well. I figured that I knew this subject so well—I had created the subject and often spoke extemporaneously about it to visitors—and only needed to decide what material to cover: the contents of material that would eventually become Markowitz (1959). I found that I had covered one-fourth of the material in three-fourths of the available time. All lectures after that are prepared for as follows: I make an outline of what I am going to say; write in the left margin of the talk, write down and circle how long I expect to take for that segment of the talk; when that is done, I go back and accumulate these segment-time units so that I know how many minutes should have accumulated by this point in the talk. Next, I divide the target total by the preliminary actual total. This gives me a ratio by which to multiply the targeted accumulated elapsed time by R to get an adjusted targeted time. This gives me a guide as to where I can amplify and where I must contract.

This has been my procedure for over half a century. I have an over 50-year-old pocket watch that facilitates this process. I no longer carry this watch except for lectures. I have deeded the watch to the UCSD "special collections" room. It will be on display along with my gold Nobel Medallion.

REFERENCES

Allais, M. 1953. "Le Comportement de l'Homme Rationnel devant le Risque: Critique des Postulats et Axiomes de l'Ecole Américaine." *Econometrica* 21(4):503–546.

Bain, A. 2004. *The Emotions and the Will.* Whitefish, MT: Kessinger Publishing. (An unabridged edition of the original 1875 publication.)

Bank of New York. 2005. New York: *New Frontiers of Risk: The 360° Risk Manager for Pensions and Nonprofits.*

Bank of New York Mellon Corporation. 2014. New York: *New Frontiers of Risk: Revisiting the 360° Manager.*

Bayes, T. 1763. "An Essay Towards Solving a Problem in the Doctrine of Chances." *Philosophical Transactions of the Royal Society of London* 53:370–418.

Berger, J. 1985. *Statistical Decision Theory and Bayesian Analysis.* 2nd ed. New York: Springer-Verlag.

Berger, J., and T. Sellke. 1987. "Testing a Point Null Hypothesis: The Irreconcilability of P Values and Evidence." *Journal of the American Statistical Association* 82:112–139.

Berkeley, G. 1734. "The Analyst." In *From Kant to Hilbert: A Source Book in the Foundations of Mathematics*, edited by W. Ewald. New York: Oxford University Press.

Bishop, E. 1967. *Foundations of Constructive Analysis.* New York: McGraw-Hill.

Brouwer, L. E. J. 1927. "On the Domains of Definition of Functions." In *From Frege to Gödel: A Source Book in Mathematical*

Logic, 1879–1931, edited by J. van Heijenoort. Lincoln, NE: To Excel Press.

Buehler, R. 1959. "Some Validity Criteria for Statistical Inferences." *Annals of Mathematical Statistics* 30:845–863.

Burali-Forti, C. 1897. "A Question on Transfinite Numbers " In *From Frege to Gödel: A Source Book in Mathematical Logic, 1879–1931*, edited by J. van Heijenoort. Lincoln, NE: To Excel Press.

Cantor, G. 1955. *Contributions to the Founding of the Theory of Transfinite Numbers*. New York: Dover Publications.

Chipman, J. S., D. MacFadden, M. K. Richter, and L. Hurwicz. 1990. *Preferences, Uncertainty, and Optimality: Essays in Honor of Leonid Hurwicz*. Boulder, CO: Westview Press.

Cohen, P. J. 1966. *Set Theory and the Continuum Hypothesis*. New York: W. A. Benjamin.

Confucius. 2014. In *The Analects*. New York: Penguin Classics. (Translated by Annping Chin.)

Crick, F. 1988. *What Mad Pursuit: A Personal View of Scientific Discovery*. New York: Basic Books.

Dantzig, G. B. 1951. "Maximization of a Linear Function of Variables Subject to Linear Inequalities." In *Activity Analysis of Production and Allocation*, edited by T. C. Koopmans, 339–347. New York: John Wiley & Sons.

_____ 1963. *Linear Programming and Extensions*. Princeton, NJ: Princeton University Press.

de Finetti, B. 1968. "Probability: Interpretations." In *International Encyclopedia of the Social Sciences*. New York: Macmillan.

DeGroot, M. H. 1970. *Optimal Statistical Decisions*. New York: McGraw-Hill.

Descartes, R. 1968. *Discourse on Method and the Meditations*. Bungay, Suffolk, England: Richard Clay (The Chaucer Press), Ltd. (First published in 1641.)

_____. 1993. *Meditations on First Philosophy*. 3rd ed. Indianapolis, IN: Hackett Publishing Company. (First published in 1641.)

Edwards, W., H. Lindman, and L. J. Savage. 1963. "Bayesian Statistical Inference for Psychological Research." *Psychological Research* 70(3):193–242.

Einstein, A. 2007. "Albert Einstein: Geometry and Experience (1921)." In *Beyond Geometry: Classic Papers from Riemann to Einstein*, edited by P. Pesic. Mineola, NY: Dover Publications. (First published in 1921.)

Einstein, A., and L. Infeld. 1938. *The Evolution of Physics: The Growth of Ideas from Early Concepts to Relativity and Quanta*. New York: Simon and Schuster.

Ellsberg, D. 1961. "Risk, Ambiguity, and the Savage Axioms." *Quarterly Journal of Economics* 75(4):643–669.

Ewald, W. 1996. *From Kant to Hilbert: A Source Book in the Foundations of Mathematics*. 2 vols. Vol. 1. New York: Oxford University Press.

Fishburn, P. C. 1970. *Utility Theory for Decision Making*. New York: John Wiley & Sons.

Fisher, R. A. 1930. "Inverse Probability." *Mathematical Proceedings of the Cambridge Philosophical Society* 26(4):528–535.

_____ 1950. *Statistical Methods for Research Workers*. 13th ed, *Biological Monographs and Manuals, 5*. London: Oliver and Boyd.

_____ 1960. *The Design of Experiments*. Edinburgh: Oliver and Boyd.

Fraenkel, A. A. 1922. "The Notion 'Definite' and the Independence of the Axiom of Choice." In *From Frege to Gödel: A Source Book in Mathematical Logic, 1879–1931*, edited by J. van Heijenoort. Lincoln, NE: To Excel Press.

Fréchet, M. 1904. "Sur Les Opérations Linéaires." *Transactions of the American Mathematical Society* 5:493–499.

Friedman, M., and L. J. Savage. 1948. "The Utility Analysis of Choices Involving Risk." *Journal of Political Economy* 56:279–304.

Frege, G. 1879. "*Begriffsschrift*, A Formula Language, Modeled Upon That of Arithmetic, for Pure Thought." In *From Frege to Gödel: A Source Book in Mathematical Logic, 1879–1931*, edited by J. van Heijenoort. Lincoln, NE: To Excel Press.

Gödel, K. 1931. "On Formally Undecidable Propositions of *Principia Mathematica* and Related Systems I." In *From Frege to Gödel: A Source Book in Mathematical Logic, 1879–1931*, edited by J. van Heijenoort. Lincoln, NE: To Excel Press.

Goodall, J. 1986. *The Chimpanzees of Gombe: Patterns of Behavior.* Cambridge, MA: Belknap Press.

_____ 2000. *In the Shadow of Man.* New York: Houghton Mifflin Harcourt.

Goodkin, M. 2012. *The Wrong Answer Faster: The Inside Story of Making the Machine That Trades Trillions.* Hoboken, NJ: John Wiley & Sons.

Halmos, P. R. 1974. *Measure Theory.* New York: Springer-Verlag.

Hamilton, A., J. Madison, and J. Jay. 2014. *The Federalist Papers.* Mineola, NY: Dover Publications. (First published in 1788.)

Hausdorff, F. 1957. *Set Theory.* New York: Chelsea Publishing Company.

Hausner, M. 1954. "Multidimensional Utilities." In *Decision Processes*, edited by R. M. Thrall, C. H. Coombs, and R. L. Davis, 167–180. New York: John Wiley & Sons.

Heyting, A. 1956. *Intuitionism: An Introduction.* Amsterdam: North-Holland Publishing Company.

_____, ed. 1959. *Constructivity in Mathematics.* Amsterdam: North-Holland Publishing Company.

Hilbert, D. 1927. "The Foundations of Mathematics." In *From Frege to Gödel: A Source Book in Mathematical Logic, 1879–1931*, edited by J. van Heijenoort. Lincoln, NE: To Excel Press.

_____ 1971. *Foundations of Geometry*. 2nd ed. La Salle, IL: Open Court Publishing Company. (First published in 1899.)

Hildreth, C. 1963. "Bayesian Statisticians and Remote Clients." *Econometrica* 31(3):422–438.

Horská, A. 2014. *Where Is the Gödel-Point Hiding: Gentzen's Consistency Proof of 1936 and His Representation of Constructive Ordinals*. New York: Springer Publishing Company.

Hume, D. 1962. *A Treatise of Human Nature Book I: Of the Understanding*. Cleveland, OH: World Publishing Company. (First published in 1739.)

_____ 1983. *An Enquiry Concerning the Principles of Morals*. Indianapolis, IN: Hackett Publishing Company. (First published in 1751.)

_____ 2009. *A Treatise of Human Nature*. Dublin: Merchant Books. (An unabridged edition of the original 1740 publication.)

Ifrah, G. 2000. *The Universal History of Numbers: From Prehistory to the Invention of the Computer*. New York: John Wiley & Sons.

James, W. 1923. *The Varieties of Religious Experience*. New York: Longmans, Green and Co. (First published in 1902.)

_____ 1980. *The Principles of Psychology*. Vol. One. New York: Dover Publications. (First published in 1890.)

Jeffreys, H. 1939. *Theory of Probability*. 2nd ed. (1948). New York: Oxford University Press.

Kamke, E. 1950. *Theory of Sets*. New York: Dover Publications.

Kanamori, A. 2009. *The Higher Infinite: Large Cardinals in Set Theory from Their Beginnings*. 2nd ed. New York: Springer.

Kant, I. 1943. *Critique of Pure Reason*. Revised ed. New York: Willey Book Co. (First published in 1781.)

Kelley, J. L. 1955. *General Topology*. New York: Litton Educational Publishing.

Kendall, M. 1994. *Kendall's Advanced Theory of Statistics*. Edited by A. Stuart and K. Ord. 6th ed. New York: Halsted Press

Keynes, J. M. 2008. *A Treatise on Probability*. Available at www.bnpublishing.com. (First published in 1920.)

Kleene, S. C. 1971. *Introduction to Metamathematics*. Groningen, Netherlands: Wolters-Noordhoff Publishing.

Knight, F. H. 1921. *Risk, Uncertainty and Profit*. Boston: Houghton Mifflin Company.

Kolmogorov, A. N. 1950. *Foundations of the Theory of Probability*. New York: Chelsea Publishing Company. (Originally published in 1933 in German by Springer, Berlin.)

Lam, W., H. M. Markowitz, and S. P. McFarland. 2015. "The Likelihood of Small Cap Premium Distribution." Available at SSRN: https://ssrn.com/abstract=2353134 or http://dx.doi.org/10.2139/ssrn.2353134.

Lebesgue, H. 1902. "Int'egrale, Longueur, Aire." Ph.D. thesis, Université de Paris. Milan: Bernandon de C. Rebeschini.

Lindley, D. V. 1957. "A Statistical Paradox." *Biometrika* 44(1–2):187–192.

_____ 1972. *Bayesian Statistics, A Review*. Philadelphia: Society for Industrial and Applied Mathematics.

Lo, A. W. 2017. *Adaptive Markets: Financial Evolution at the Speed of Thought*. Princeton, NJ: Princeton University Press.

Lo, A. W., and M. T. Mueller. 2010. "Warning: Physics Envy May Be Hazardous to Your Wealth." *Journal of Investment Management* (Second Quarter 2010).

MacKay, C. 2013. *Extraordinary Popular Delusions and the Madness of Crowds*: Maestro Reprints. (First published in 1841.)

MacTutor History of Mathematics Archive. 1999b. "Pierre-Simon Laplace." University of St. Andrews, Scotland, Last Modified January 1999.

———— 2003a. "Luitzen Egbertus Jan Brouwer." University of St. Andrews, Scotland, Last Modified October 2003.

———— 2003b. "Kurt Gödel." University of St. Andrews, Scotland, Last Modified October 2003.

———— 2005. "Hermann Klaus Hugo Weyl." University of St. Andrews, Scotland, Last Modified August 2005.

Markowitz, H. M. 1952. "Portfolio Selection." *Journal of Finance* 7 (1):77–91.

———— 1959. *Portfolio Selection: Efficient Diversification of Investments.* 2nd ed. New York: John Wiley & Sons.

Markowitz, H. M., A. Tessitore, A. Tessitore, and N. Usmen. 2014. "The Likelihood of Various Return Distributions." In *Risk-Return Analysis: The Theory and Practice of Rational Investing*, Vol. I, by Harry Markowtiz, 149–194. New York: McGraw-Hill.

Markowitz, H. M., and N. Usmen. 1996a. "The Likelihood of Various Stock Market Return Distributions, Part 1: Principles of Inference." *Journal of Risk and Uncertainty* 13:207–219.

———— 1996b. "The Likelihood of Various Stock Market Return Distributions, Part 2: Empirical Results." *Journal of Risk and Uncertainty* 13:221–247.

Nash, J. 1950. "Equilibrium Points in N-Person Games." *Proceedings of the National Academy of Sciences* 36(1):49–49.

Newell, A, J. C. Shaw, and H. A. Simon. 1957. "Empirical Explorations of the Logic Theory Machine: A Case Study in Heuristic." Western Joint Computer Conference Proceedings, Los Angeles, CA.

———— 1958. "Chess-Playing Programs of Complexity." *IBM J Research and Development* 2(4):320–335.

Newton, I. 1966. *Principia*. Berkeley, CA: University of California Press. (First published, in Latin, in 1687.) Translated into English by A. Motte in 1729.

Neyman, J., and E. S. Pearson. 1933. "On the Problem of the Most Efficient Tests of Statistical Hypotheses." *Philosophical Transactions of the Royal Society of London* 231:289–337.

Nobel Foundation. 1990. "Les Prix Nobel: The Nobel Prizes 1990." Stockholm, Sweden.

Odean, T. 1999. "Do Investors Trade Too Much?" *American Economic Review* 89:1279–1298.

Peano, G. 1889. "The Principles of Arithmetic, Presented by a New Method." In *From Frege to Gödel: A Source Book in Mathematical Logic, 1879–1931*, edited by J. van Heijenoort. Lincoln, NE: To Excel Press.

Peirce, C. 1955a. "The Essentials of Pragmatism." In *The Philosophical Writings of Peirce*, edited by J. Buchler. New York: Dover Publications. (First published in 1907.)

———— 1955b. *The Philosophical Writings of Peirce*. New York: Dover Publications.

———— 1955c. "Pragmatism in Retrospect: A Last Formulation." In *The Philosophical Writings of Peirce*, edited by J. Buchler. New York: Dover Publications. (First published in 1908.)

Pesic, P., ed. 2007. *Beyond Geometry: Classic Papers from Reimann to Einstein*. Mineola, NY: Dover Publications.

Poincaré, H. 2012. *Science and Hypothesis*. London: Forgotten Books. (First published in 1902.)

Popper, K. 1963. *Conjectures and Refutations*. London: Routledge.

Riemann, B. 2007. "Bernhard Riemann: On the Hypotheses That Lie at the Foundations of Geometry (1854)." In *Beyond Geometry: Classic Papers from Riemann to Einstein*, edited by P. Pesic. Mineola, NY: Dover Publications.

Robinson, A. 1974. *Non-Standard Analysis*. New York: American Elsevier Publishing Company.

Rubin, R. E., A. Greenspan, A. Levitt, and B. Born. 1999. "Hedge Funds, Leverage and the Lessons of Long-Term Capital

Management." The President's Working Group on Financial Markets.

Russell, B. 1908. "Mathematical Logic as Based on the Theory of Types." In *From Frege to Gödel: A Source Book in Mathematical Logic, 1879–1931*, edited by J. van Heijenoort. Lincoln, NE: To Excel Press.

Savage, L. J. 1954. *The Foundations of Statistics*. 2nd rev. ed. (1971). New York: Dover Publications.

Scarf, H. E. 1973. *The Computation of Economic Equilibria*. New Haven, CT: Yale University Press.

Skolem, T. 1922. "Some Remarks on Axiomatized Set Theory." In *From Frege to Gödel: A Source Book in Mathematical Logic, 1879–1931*, edited by J. van Heijenoort. Lincoln, NE: To Excel Press.

Smith, A. 2003. *The Wealth of Nations*. New York: Bantam Classics. (First published in 1776.)

Tarski, A. 1995. *Introduction to Logic and to the Methodology of Deductive Sciences*. Mineola, NY: Dover Publications.

Thrall, R. M. 1954. "Applications of Multidimensional Utility Theory." In *Decision Processes*, edited by R. M. Thrall, C. H. Coombs, and R. L. Davis, 181–186. New York: John Wiley & Sons.

van Heijenoort, J., ed. 1967. *From Frege to Gödel: A Source Book in Mathematical Logic, 1879–1931*. Lincoln, NE: To Excel Press.

Von Neumann, J. 1945–1946. "A Model of General Economic Equilibrium." *Review of Economic Studies* 13(1):1–9.

Von Neumann, J., and O. Morgenstern. 1944. *Theory of Games and Economic Behavior*. 3rd ed. Princeton, NJ: Princeton University Press.

Whitehead, A., and B. Russell. 1970. *Principia Mathematica to *56*. London: The Syndics of the Cambridge University Press. (First published in 1910.)

Wikipedia Contributors. 2019a. "Brouwer Fixed-Point Theorem." Wikipedia, The Free Encyclopedia. Last modified, June 18, 2019.

_____ 2019b. "Hilbert's Problems." Wikipedia, The Free Encyclopedia. Last modified, August 5, 2019.

Williams, J. B. 1997. *The Theory of Investment Value*. Flint Hill, VA: Fraser Publishing Co. (First published in 1938.)

Zellner, A. 1971. *An Introduction to Bayesian Inference in Econometrics*. New York: John Wiley & Sons.

Zermelo, E. 1908. "Investigations in the Foundations of Set Theory I." In *From Frege to Gödel: A Source Book in Mathematical Logic, 1879–1931*, edited by J. van Heijenoort. Lincoln, NE: To Excel Press.

INDEX

AA. *See* Application area
"About the Things We May Doubt"
   (Descartes), 4–7
Absolute power, 277
Accept regions, 244–245, 247–248
Action
   altruistic, 26
   belief in relation to, 59–61, 197
   information into, 1–2
   of specialists, 61
   working hypotheses guiding, 13
Acton, Lord, 277
AI. *See* Artificial Intelligence
Algebraic structure, 190–191
Alternative universe (AU)
   exploration in, 71–75
   learning in, 77–78
   perceptions in, 76–77
   physics in, 71, 72–73
   sensations in, 75–76
   time in, 77
Altruistic actions, 26
Alzheimer's, 11
Analyses. *See also* Mean-variance analysis
   economic, 33–39
   infinite-dimensional utility, 190
   many-period, xiii
   Nonstandard, 190
   single-period, xiii
   statistical, 242–244
Analytic geometry, 6
Ancient arithmetic, 99
Anomalies, 32
Application area (AA), 256–257
Approximation
   Axiom III judgment and, 217–221
   of MVA to EU, 38, 215–217
Archaeology, 99
Archimedean axioms, 217–220
Archimedes, 185
Aristotle
   on deductive reasoning, 19
   disciple of, 4
   on *eudaimonia*, 28

Hume compared to, 196
   on inductive reasoning, 19
   law of the excluded middle by, 150–152
   Nicomachean Ethics by, 196
   Organon of, 19, 177–178
   Plato debating with, 84–85
   Posterior Analytics by, 19, 120, 124
   Prior Analytics by, 19, 120, 124
   on self-interest in society, 276–277
   syllogism of, 80–81, 178–181
Arithmetic
   ancient, 99
   finite cardinal, 91–95
   finite ordinal, 95–97
   transfinite cardinal, 108–109
   transfinite ordinal, 113–114
Arrow, Kenneth, 142
Artificial Intelligence (AI), 172
Asset classes, 39
Assets under management (AUM), 37
AU. *See* Alternative universe
AUM. *See* Assets under management
Awareness, 131–132
Axiom I
   comments on, 209–210
   explanation of, 208–209
   values assigned to, 207
Axiom II
   comments on, 210–211
   explanation of, 209
   problems with, 229–232
   values assigned to, 207
Axiom III
   explanation of, 209
   judgment and approximation regarding,
     217–221
   values assigned to, 207–208
Axiom IV
   explanation of, 209
   values assigned to, 208
Axiom of choice. *See also* Zermelo,
     Fraenkel, Choice axioms
   defining, 161–162, 281–282
   Trichotomy equivalent to, 162–163

297

ABOUT THE AUTHOR

Harry M. Markowitz is a Nobel Laureate and the father of Modern Portfolio Theory. Named "Man of the Century" by *Pensions & Investments* magazine, he is a recipient of the prestigious John von Neumann Theory Prize for his work in portfolio theory, sparse matrix techniques, and the SIMSCRIPT programming language.